Academic Librarianship

Beta Phi Mu Scholars Series

Founded in 1948, Beta Phi Mu is the international library and information studies honor society. Its mission is to recognize and encourage scholastic achievement among library and information studies students.

The Beta Phi Mu Scholars series publishes significant contributions and substantive advances in the field of library and information science. Series editor Andrea Falcone is committed to presenting work which reflects Beta Phi Mu's commitments to scholarship, leadership, and service. The series fosters creative, innovative, and well-articulated works that members of the field will find influential.

Recently published titles in the series are:

Book Banning in 21st-Century America by Emily J. M. Knox
Young Adult Literature, Libraries, and Conservative Activism by Loretta M. Gaffney
School Librarianship: Past, Present, and Future Edited by Susan W. Alman
Six Issues Facing Libraries Today: Critical Perspectives by John Budd
Access to Information, Technology, and Justice: A Critical Intersection by Ursula Gorham
Academic Library Metamorphosis and Regeneration by Marcy Simons
Collaborations for Student Success: How Librarians and Student Affairs Work Together to Enrich Learning by Dallas Long
Partners in Teaching and Learning: Coordinating a Successful Academic Library by Melissa Mallon
Academic Librarianship: Anchoring the Profession in Contribution, Scholarship, and Service by Marcy Simons

Academic Librarianship

Anchoring the Profession in Contribution, Scholarship, and Service

Marcy Simons

ROWMAN & LITTLEFIELD
Lanham • Boulder • New York • London

Published by Rowman & Littlefield
An imprint of The Rowman & Littlefield Publishing Group, Inc.
4501 Forbes Boulevard, Suite 200, Lanham, Maryland 20706
www.rowman.com

6 Tinworth Street, London SE11 5AL, United Kingdom

Copyright © 2021 by The Rowman & Littlefield Publishing Group, Inc.

All rights reserved. No part of this book may be reproduced in any form or by any electronic or mechanical means, including information storage and retrieval systems, without written permission from the publisher, except by a reviewer who may quote passages in a review.

British Library Cataloguing in Publication Information Available

Library of Congress Cataloging-in-Publication Data

Names: Simons, Marcy, author.
Title: Academic librarianship : anchoring the profession in contribution, scholarship, and service / Marcy Simons.
Description: Lanham : Rowman & Littlefield, [2021] | Series: Beta Phi Mu scholars series | Includes bibliographical references and index. | Summary: "This book is needed now as a response to how much has changed in academic librarianship as a profession (from the smallest academic libraries to large research libraries). Topics covered include: state of the profession of librarianship today, status of librarians, how are librarians conducting research, and more"—Provided by publisher.
Identifiers: LCCN 2020056990 (print) | LCCN 2020056991 (ebook) | ISBN 9781538183595 (paper) | ISBN 9781538136218 (ebook)
Subjects: LCSH: Academic libraries—United States. | Academic librarians—Professional ethics—United States.
Classification: LCC Z675.U5 S5528 2021 (print) | LCC Z675.U5 (ebook) | DDC 027.70973—dc23
LC record available at https://lccn.loc.gov/2020056990
LC ebook record available at https://lccn.loc.gov/2020056991

Contents

Preface		vii
Acknowledgments		ix
1	The Profession of Librarianship	1
2	The Question of Status	17
3	Anchoring the Profession in Scholarship	29
4	Anchored in Service	43
5	Education	57
6	A Path Forward	75
Bibliography		91
Index		103
About the Author		105

Preface

Higher education and the academic libraries within them are undergoing change at a remarkable rate, and in 2020—just when we thought we understood what sorts of disruptions we should be preparing for—a novel coronavirus proved once again that we have no idea where the next driver for change will come from.

This book explores the history of the profession of academic librarianship. The research came from a place of curiosity—a quest to understand why we seem to be divided on so many issues that are hallmarks of the profession. Things like the "MLS from an ALA-accredited program" requirement, faculty status and the myriad of considerations that go into it, contributions, service, and research round out the top five standards that have been questioned in recent years. Along the way, it became clear that the arguments both for and against these standards arise from some very strong and long-held beliefs and experiences.

The first chapter creates a framework for the profession of librarianship. That framework contains the definition of the profession, the emergence of librarianship as a profession, and standards that define status. It also describes professional contribution, research, service, and education and takes a look at the future.

From that framework, the next chapter moves to the question of status. Early on—very early in fact (1891)—university professors and others supported faculty status and tenure for academic librarians. Despite a century of debate, questions remain as to whether faculty status is both attainable and appropriate or not.

Chapter 3 examines research within the profession of library and information science specifically. Because *contribution to the profession* is one of three domains for evaluation in the academy, how do librarians fare? Early on, discussions among those in higher education indicated that librarians conducting research had "limited value." Thanks to the emergence of scientific methodology for library and information science research in 1921 and the addition of the Association of College and Reference Librarians in 1940, that opinion has changed. We still have work to do, though.

A second domain for evaluation is *service*, so chapter 4 takes a closer look at definitions, opportunities, professional associations, and other measures.

Early on in this research process, it became clear that education was at the center of the debate around our roles and our status. The findings here include new questions, yet they also offer hope.

And finally, where do we go from here? The last chapter examines the trends and issues facing twenty-first-century academic libraries and delves into some of the suggestions and proposals made over the years to help us find a new path forward.

I continue to believe that a regeneration of our profession is happening. There are passionate people committed to ensuring continuous improvement, excellence, and commitment.

Acknowledgments

Instead of believing the old adage "curiosity killed the cat," I choose to believe that curiosity is everything. It drives lifelong learning and the creation of knowledge. Having the opportunity to pursue my curiosity within my profession continues to be most rewarding and fulfilling. I will always be grateful to my institution, library leadership, and colleagues I work with who encourage and support this curiosity.

As always, I have to acknowledge and thank my family—my siblings, my children, and my husband—for their unwavering love, support, and encouragement, especially during this past year. While trying to work, conduct research, and write, I experienced the highest of highs with the birth of my first grandson, Knixon Kyle, and the lowest of lows with the devastating loss of my mother. Every day, my family shows me that together we can do anything.

Chapter One

The Profession of Librarianship

"A librarian's work is cerebral and indeterminate, rarely being the application of some fixed formula or procedure. Each new client or new problem is a new intellectual challenge that is met with a fresh, inventive response—not by reference to some canonical 'body of knowledge.' A librarian's work cannot be disaggregated into the convenient series of tasks so beloved of work analysts. A librarian's work is far closer to the faculty's teaching and research than to anything subject to industrial work analysis. Like other knowledge professionals—surgeons, lawyers, economists, scientists, professors—librarians are intimately involved with the interactive dynamics and unpredictable outcomes of living systems, for example, other people and society as a whole."—Allen B. Veaner

Librarianship as a profession has been questioned almost as long as librarianship has *been* a profession. This book stems from a desire to figure out once and for all answers to the questions of "librarianship as a profession," specifically academic librarianship. Because questions about our status as professionals affects us all, this book focuses on librarians within the academy and higher education. Librarians appear to have very clearly defined expectations for achieving professional status: a "terminal degree," research, contribution, and service. Not so easy, as there is much to be considered: questions of when librarianship became a profession, as well as issues of power, prestige, gender, labor, and technology. One could make it their life's work to try to make sense of it all and still not have all the answers. That is what I have learned in trying to identify, define, describe, propose, and ultimately anchor a way for this profession to move forward.

Like any good researcher, I began this study with a framework. The framework included finding answers to these initial questions:

- What are the official criteria to define a profession?

- Who or what determines that someone is a professional?
- When did librarianship emerge as a profession?
- What are the formal educational requirements assigned to our profession?
- What are the professional (and nonprofessional) aspects and functions of academic librarianship?
- How do we maintain our status? (Are there accreditations, certifications, and standards in place to guide us?)
- How do we compare with other professions, and do those professions experience the same questions about their status that librarians do?

Very quickly it became apparent that there would be no easy answers. For example, as this chapter shows, there does not appear to be one main definition of *profession*; people don't agree that the criteria to define *librarianship* are the right ones; and standards for education don't have consensus.

Many before now have attempted to answer these and similar questions: There was no shortage of information in a literature review. For example, the search terms "librarianship as a profession" produced 22,630 results in a standard database search. Some of that information specifically came from the *Library, Information Science and Technology Abstracts*, with a results list including articles, reviews, newspaper articles, dissertations, text resources, books, conference proceedings, and data sets, just to name a few. There has been a lot written, shared, talked about, challenged, and "proven" about librarianship as a profession.

In today's climate, particularly regarding social justice, there are questions about labor, diversity, "vocational awe," and gender. In addition, previous illusions to our professional identity have been shattered, specifically icons like Melville Dewey and Andrew Carnegie. For example, a 2018 *Washington Post* article notes that Carnegie's generosity came with strings (Mitchell 2018), and in 2019, an "American Library Association [ALA] resolution points to Dewey's history of discriminatory and predatory behavior" to justify stripping Dewey's name from the association's top award (Katz 2019).

Today many voices are asking interesting and sometimes difficult questions. Some of those are offered here for the reader to consider and discuss; you can come to your own conclusions. Ultimately, from my perspective, this book accepts the notion of academic librarianship as a profession worthy of the word while acknowledging areas where there is more work to be done. And it all starts with research.

HISTORICAL REVIEW AND DEFINITIONS

Some brief history is necessary to set the stage for creating an informed framework. A. K. Mukherjee (1966) notes in *Librarianship, Its Philosophy and History*, librarianship

> claims to be an ancient occupation dating back to the days of the Assyrian King Assurbanipal, who lived from 668 to 631 B.C. From the days of this librarian-king, through Zenodotus of Ephesus, the curator of the Alexandrian Library, to the modern age, there have been centuries of different culture periods in human civilization, extinct and extant, assiduously endeavouring to preserve their cultural heritage, for the use of the then present generation and for posterity.

More detailed information on the history of libraries is provided in *Readings in Library History* (Dunlap 1972), *Foundations of Library and Information Science* (Rubin 2016), and *Libraries and Librarianship in the West: A Brief History* (Jackson 1974), just to name a few. All the historical reports have a shared understanding of "library" as a cultural institution; a place where information is both created and preserved; and a place that requires people (for now—AI could change everything, but that discussion is saved for another chapter) to care for, maintain, organize, categorize—and revolutionize—everything.

That is a pretty bold statement, but at the heart of education lies exactly that opportunity. Every major institution of higher learning has a tagline reinforcing that notion. For example, at the University of Notre Dame, all are encouraged to be a "force for good in the world"; at MIT, the "community is driven by a shared purpose: to make a better world through education, research, and innovation"; and New York University strives to be an "innovator in higher education, reaching out to an emerging middle class, embracing an urban identity and professional focus, and promoting a global vision." It would stand to reason, then, that academic libraries, and by extension the people who work in them, have a role to play in that revolution.

Going back to the framework, there are two important historical implications: consideration of the word *profession* and "librarianship as a profession." First, let's look at the word *professional*. In "Professing Professionalism: Bureaucratization and Deprofessionalization in the Academy," Keith Roberts and Karen Donahue (2012) cite Ballantine (1997) in their analysis of professional standards and what differentiates them from occupations. Their list of factors includes the following:

1. Mastery of specialized theory. The professional must master a body of rather sophisticated and abstract theory and knowledge to perform the tasks associated with the profession.

2. Autonomy and control of one's work and how one's work is performed.
3. Motivation through intrinsic rewards and the interests of clients—which take precedence over the professional's self-interests.
4. Commitment to the profession as a career and to the service objectives of the organization for which one works.
5. Sense of community, feelings of collegiality with others in the profession, and accountability to those colleagues.
6. Self-monitoring and regulation by the profession through ethical and professional standards and a detailed code of ethics.

Their list matches closely with a list W. H. Cowley provides in his 1928 book *The Profession of Librarianship*, as expressed in 1915 by Dr. Abraham Flexner, an authority on medical education:

1. Professions involve essentially intellectual operations with large individual responsibility.
2. They derive their raw material from science and learning.
3. This material they work up to a practical and definite end.
4. They possess an educationally communicable technique.
5. They tend to self-organize.
6. They are becoming increasingly altruistic in motivation.

In addition, Cowley (1928) offers a second list of criteria for consideration, this one from another educator, President Emeritus Charles F. Thwing of Western Reserve University, who suggested that the "permanent and distinguishing characteristics of a profession" are the following:

1. Money making is regarded as a condition, not as an aim.
2. The members of a profession have a sense of brotherhood among themselves.
3. They perform a public service.
4. They possess certain standards of entrance.
5. There exists a body of literature concerning the profession.

Library and Information Science Research: Perspectives and Strategies for Improvement provides another offering of attributes of a profession. That seminal work describes the difference between a discipline and a profession. A discipline, Hernon (1991) says, includes nine attributes:

1. A recognized area of study.
2. Departmental status, autonomy, and formal recognition in academe.
3. A substantial body of knowledge and theory.

4. A "common state of mind," including a sense of agreement on areas of inquiry and methods for studying problems and a common belief that extending the discipline's insights is a worthy endeavor.
5. A belief that the continued development of the discipline depends on the generation of basic and applied research.
6. A number of people, well known within and outside the discipline, revered as contributors to knowledge, research, and practice.
7. Support from a national learned society.
8. Its age.
9. A number of people in its study.

He then offers yet another description of a profession, this one from Dr. Michael B. Spring, who proposes that a profession consists of the following:

1. A body of knowledge and theory essential for professionals to master.
2. A knowledge base resulting from prolonged study of training or socialization in the profession.
3. Application of knowledge and service to human problems.
4. Service orientation "based on some theoretical structure or department of learning" and "practical experience."
5. A demand for service and a willingness to help others.
6. Recognition of practitioners as professionals and as meeting a need; "practitioners are clearly distinguished from non-practitioners."
7. Training and education for new professionals.
8. Professional organizations.
9. Professional functions and set norms of professional conduct identified by professional organizations.
10. Impartial services to the public rendered by practitioners.
11. Esteem for the profession from society.
12. Sense of community, commitment, and autonomy—a belief that one's work is a lifelong calling and does not require supervision from someone outside the work group or profession.
13. A relationship with academe.
14. Professional-client relationship.
15. Expected level of educational achievement.
16. Expected norms for entrance into the profession.
17. A system of rewards.
18. Certification of competence and high level of professional standards.
19. Criteria for evaluating achievement and excellence.
20. A "full-time" and "life-time commitment" to practice the profession.
21. Practitioners' "monopoly on the right to deliver their particular service" and belief "that only practitioners are competent to judge the services delivered." (Hernon 1991)

Just to cover our bases, here are the Webster's Dictionary definitions of *profession*:

a   a calling requiring specialized knowledge and often long and intensive academic preparation

b   a principal calling, vocation, or employment

c   the whole body of persons engaged in a calling

Now, Cowley also notes that the word *profession* was greatly abused. He writes that with the "rapid development of our industrial civilization, engineering soon became recognized as a profession, and now almost every type of work above the trades is at one time or another claimed as a profession" (Cowley 1928). His aim is to point out why librarianship was then an accepted profession and to outline the general characteristics that make it so. He says there are "no natural measuring sticks" to help understand why some jobs are considered professional while others are not (for example, law but not business; ministry but not farming) (Cowley 1928). Finally, William Henry (1922) notes that the "professional men and women must everywhere and always be the guardians, guides, advisers, and directors of the people. Perhaps no other mark so distinguishes the professions."

How do we use all these proposed definitions and attributes to determine that academic librarianship specifically is a profession? To do that, we need to go back to the beginning of librarianship. In 1938, A. F. Kuhlman wrote an article called "Librarianship as a Profession" for the *Peabody Journal of Education*. In it, he discusses the changing concepts of librarianship, as at the time it was an "emerging profession." The purpose of the paper, he says, is to "indicate in what respects and to what extent librarianship can now be regarded as a profession" (Kuhlman 1938).

Using Dr. Abraham Flexner's six criteria of professions, for each one, Kulhman provides evidence for or, in some cases, work that needs to take place to say unequivocally that librarianship is a profession. For example, he notes confusion around those who were/are considered professional librarians in the early days, when everyone who worked in the library was called "librarian." The reasons for the confusion, he notes, were that "even the routine and clerical activities in a library require the most exacting attention. Skill and accuracy are indispensable. Hence, as Dr. Charles C. Williamson has pointed out, there has been a tendency for indiscriminate minds to attach to purely clerical activities the dignity and importance of library work" (Kuhlman 1938). In addition, he says, when staffs are small, everyone has to do the clerical work to keep the library open and functioning. Another point relates to the librarian's original chief function as "keeper" of books, keeping them safe and secure. Then, he notes that those early library schools did not differentiate adequately between clerical and professional activities and, finally, that the differences were not encouraged by our professional association (Kuhlman 1938). Kuhlman does note that from the mid- to late twenties through the time of his writing, much attention was given to improving library service, to the application of scientific methods, and to the requirements for more rigorous and serious learning. He concludes, "[L]ibrarianship is a profession in the making" (Kuhlman 1938).

Lester Asheim (1978) writes in his article "Librarians as Professionals" that

> librarians began to be conscious of their status and their identity as a definable calling at the same time that practitioners in many other fields were doing so. Professional associations began to appear in the latter half of the nineteenth century—the first national law association was founded in 1878; social work in 1874; and between 1864 and 1888, nine separate specialties within medicine all established associations. Even sports began to professionalize; 1876 marks the establishment not only of the ALA, but of the National League as well.

Asheim also refers to the Flexner criteria of professions, and he includes a thorough review of the way social scientists in the 1960s began to question all previous definitions of occupations and professions, noting that librarians were trying to come to terms with the discrepancies between those previously accepted definitions and what they found in theory and practice. Asheim (1978) says, "[T]here was never a doubt that professional status is what they wanted and that if there were areas in which they did not yet measure up, the logical course of action was to work to remedy these inadequacies." Asheim also points to a 1968 study by Dale Shaffer that explores the maturity of librarianship as a profession. In that study, Shaffer points out several areas where our profession differs from those more traditional (medicine, law, theology), citing specifically that no internship or student librarianship is required; not every library school was accredited by the American Library Association, and only one-third of the country's librarians were members of our association, as compared to 69 percent of physicians who were members of the American Medical Association (Shaffer 1968).

Like Asheim, William Henry (1922) notes that the

> profession of librarianship, coming to consciousness as a social need so recently as it did—fourty-six years ago—and starting without estate or tradition, has secured for itself an enviable growth and a standing in the respect of many but not of most. The marvel of it is that it has done so well. No profession perhaps has reached so high a level of intelligence and so strong a sentiment for professional preparation so early in its career as has librarianship but we must recall that we are the youngest of the group and that we progress more now in forty years than older professions did in many centuries. Our profession must continue to elevate its standards, for, like the Golden Rule it has infinite

possibilities in its reinterpretations. The profession will grow in its own self-respect and in the respect of others just as it keeps its standards almost out of reach.

A summary of those early pioneers who wrote about our profession came to positive conclusions. Not everyone, though, even in the early years, agreed that librarians were professionals. Or they noted where discrepancies needed to be addressed. Pierce Butler wrote his "Librarianship as a Profession" article for the *Library Quarterly* in October 1951, in which he summarizes ideas that he hoped would influence necessary changes. Butler (1951) writes that

> we all do believe that librarianship is a profession. We have long since come to feel that it belongs in the same category as do such vocations as medicine, law, and engineering. But our belief here is an emotional conviction rather than a rational conclusion. We can adduce neither evidence nor argument to justify our opinion. Nor shall we be able to do so until we clarify our ideas about what the essential nature of a professional is.

He says that at issue is that "anyone who worked in a library or was interested in libraries was regarded as a librarian. Hence, the organization has always been what the American Medical Association would be if it enrolled druggists, nurses, and hospital clerks as well as physicians, gave them all an equal vote, and evaded ill-advised majority decisions by political manipulations" (Butler 1951). His article notes that certification for librarians and the production of scholarship were sorely lacking.

Other authors point out some of the discrepancies of our assignment as professionals. For example, William J. Goode (1961) writes that

> in some contexts, the term "professional librarian" simply means "adequately trained." But the specific knowledge which such a librarian must possess is not clear. It is difficult to define a problem for whose solution one would uniquely go to a librarian. Lay opinion does not recognize any special talent for librarianship even among those who are about to graduate, nor is there any commonly accepted criterion by which one might judge good or poor performance by a librarian.

He concludes that the library is "viewed in part as a museum, a treasure house, but the librarian must spread a new conception, subtle and perhaps difficult to explain successfully, that the library is a gigantic reference book containing fantasy as well as fact, whose order, created by the unique professional skill of the librarian, makes it more valuable and accessible to all" (Goode 1961).

Also in 1961, Ralph H. Parker set out to identify ports of entry into librarianship because even then, librarians had become "vocally concerned with the failure of the profession to recruit outstanding young people in sufficient numbers. Efforts to correct the situation have taken various forms, including a nationwide recruiting committee, emphasis on improving the status of librarianship, and elimination of clerical aspects of professional positions, to name only a few" (Parker and Reagan 1961). Parker notes that other professionals were experiencing problems with recruitment going back to the economic depression of 1929, which led to what he calls the "psychology of exclusion." This was applied to all professions to control the number of recruits. As a result, enrollments were limited, professional schools were closed, and new ones were discouraged from opening (Parker and Reagan 1961). He cites the library profession, medicine, law, and engineering as involved in the restrictions. For more than a decade, these limitations had an impact on new graduates because library systems could not hire enough, leading many candidates to accept clerical employment, which would ultimately dilute the "professional character of positions to employ more librarians instead of clerks" (Parker and Reagan 1961).

Parker describes how the accreditation process and its changes, by 1951, led to the "idea that only a graduate program in library science could offer acceptable training," which opened "one port of entry into the profession: the accredited graduate library school" (Parker and Reagan 1961). This article provides us with important information about changes in our profession that continue to have an impact on all of us today.

By 1968, authors writing about librarianship as a profession indicated that those earlier questions still existed. Mary Lee Bundy and Paul Wasserman write in "Professionalism Reconsidered" that despite many attempts to revise and improve educational programs, expectations, and professionalization requirements, much work was left to be done. They also note a serious personnel shortage, which must be addressed through continued professionalization. They write about the "professional" through three relationships: with clients, with their institutions, and with the professional group. Looking at the librarian-client relationship, Bundy and Wasserman (1968) propose that often the librarian plays the role of a nonexpert, one who is reluctant to "assume responsibility for solving informational problems and providing unequivocal answers." Under the institutional relationship, the same argument is applied that remains today: Academic libraries belong within a larger organizational hierarchy whose standards are applied to professionals. They state, "Librarians man desks and meet schedule commitments, and in the process, deny and are denied the opportunity to care, to grow and to act professionally" (Bundy and Wasserman 1968).

Following that same line of reasoning, Orvin Lee Shiflett wrote about the origins of American academic librarianship in 1981. He details the history of higher education, and in a chapter on the scholar and the librarian, he traces the path of librarians in the academy. The emergence of research and scholarship as important aspects of the academic community led to new ways that academic librarians could provide value and service to the university. Shiflett (1981) describes new connections between academic librarians and students, such as helping them to

> cope with the masses of materials accumulated by academic libraries, offering lectures on bibliography and research methods, and generally attempting to supplement the activities of the faculty in encouraging undergraduate students to broaden their education through reading, [which] became the functions that academic librarians came to identify as their functions in American higher education.

PROFESSIONALIZATION AND LABOR THEORY

In 1983, Michael Winter wrote an Occasional Paper on the professionalization of librarianship. His perspective was on the development of the library occupation within sociological approaches to professionalization, and he notes that the "great movements of industrialization" brought with them an increase in the number and types of occupations, creating a previously "unknown complexity in the social division of labor" (Winter 1983).

Thus, the

> information fields emerged as a result of the increase of complexity in the division of labor, and a parallel increase in the quantity and complexity of the knowledge—practical, technical, and theoretical—and available information that are put to work in typical occupational routines. . . . [L]ibrarians and other information specialists have found that work increasingly requires a commitment to the acquisition of technical skills and the mastery of theoretical principles. (Winter 1983)

Winter (1983) discusses these changes through the eyes of philosophers and sociologists, pointing out that

> [s]ocioeconomic complexity requires a parallel complexity of organization, and this in turn requires formalization, hierarchical arrangement, or rationalization—and the key to this use of the term "rationalization" is the subjection of individual impulse to organizational imperatives. By individualizing persons as workers, by stressing the uniqueness of each occupation's contribution to our social and economic welfare, advanced industrial society had nurtured within itself a counterthrust to the advance of bureaucratization. The more concerned we are with our individuality and our personal occupational achievements, the less likely we are to appreciate being subjected to formal bureaucratic routines. And yet the more individualized we become, the greater is the need for authoritative mechanisms of social order to coordinate social action.

What does that have to do with librarianship? Winter (1983) questions our professionalization not by asking "is it or is it not a profession? but rather: What degree of professionalization has a certain group shown?" To answer, he proposes the use of a composite model that builds on the trait and functionalist models proposed by social theorists. This model considers the connection between professional associations, schools, the institutionalization of those traits, and the autonomy inherent within them.

Even though he doesn't ultimately answer the question, his work provides another perspective from which the question of our professionalization should be considered. For, as he notes, the sociology of labor born of the nineteenth century created the need for and importance of the "professional association, licensing procedures and ethics codes, formal training programs, legitimate monopolies over certain bodies of knowledge, service orientation, and community recognition. All these legitimate the professional's freedom and protect it, enabling the practitioner to respond to external pressure without submitting to the control of outside agents" (Winter 1983). This leads to distinctions of class, tied up in rights, privileges, prestige, and power.

Between Winter's discussion of the sociology of labor in the 1980s and the early 2000s, there wasn't much else attributed to the concept of labor. More recently, though, we are beginning to see some very interesting research of the concept in relation to "profession" and academic librarianship. For example, at CAPAL18 (Canadian Association of Professional Academic Librarians, 2018), Jane Schmidt, a liaison librarian at Ryerson University, challenged ways in which "bullshit" has manifested itself in the academic library. Schmidt made some compelling arguments and offered concrete solutions for pushing back. Her bibliography includes the discovery of "labor" as a concept currently making its way through the literature. She specifically looks at the work of Emily Drabinski (2016) in "Valuing Professionalism: Discourse as Professional Practice" and Lisa Sloniowski (2016) in "Affective Labor, Resistance, and the Academic Librarian." Drabinski starts out the way this chapter does—by looking at the definitions of *profession*. From her perspective, professionals approach discussions of what they *are* rather than what they *do*. Her article describes an inherent problem of professionalization: They produce "hierarchies infused with power and privilege" (Drabinski 2016). She notes that the literature focuses on the "'crisis' of professional status," which is "understood as a status achieved once and for all, requiring consolidation and protection through urgent action on the part of librarians" (Drabinski 2016). She proposes instead that "while Professionalism is a Core Value, the value is not fixed; instead, Professionalism is continually produced and reproduced in the library discourse, always in response to an urgent present or impending future that requires a new form of consolidation" (Drabinski 2016). She concludes that the advantages accrued through professionalization produce exclusion and inequity. The perspective that professionalization is exclusionary is not new, but it has made a renewed comeback in today's discussions of embracing inclusion globally.

Another perspective of labor is offered by Lisa Sloniowski, who wrote the article "Affective Labor, Resistance, and the Academic Librarian" in 2016 to "explore the gendered dimensions of affective labor." She describes the exclusionary practice of professionalism, as academic librarians suffer from lack of prestige and recognition when compared to faculty. She notes many issues we can all relate to still today: cuts to library operating budgets mean that most libraries operate without enough librarians; increases in enrollment and demand to offer new digital services in both collections and teaching add pressure; and the last two decades have included "significant existential and institutional crisis" (Sloniowski 2016). In addition, Sloniowski says, the perception of faculty colleagues of a lower status means librarians tend not to be considered for higher-level university service opportunities and are viewed as support workers. More about the perception of university colleagues and status is discussed in the next chapter.

The question remains: how do we get our university colleagues to understand that not only do we produce our own knowledge but also that we are a key piece of the production of knowledge in higher education? Sloniowski provides an interesting look at this through the likes of Michel Foucaut and Jacques Derrida. She writes,

> In *Archive Fever*, Derrida (1998) argued that there is no political power without control of the archive, and that the technologies of archivization (which are largely created by librarians and archivists) produce, as well as store the historical record (pp. 4, 17). Foucault (1972) suggests, in *The Archaeology of Knowledge*, that enunciability itself depends on the archive: what can and cannot be said is predicated on what we preserve and how we make it available (p. 129). And yet, librarians struggle to find the time to write and theorize intensively about the social and political dimensions of libraries, archives, and the technologies of archivization. By not publishing and presenting on these issues to other scholars—issues that we have intimate and practical engagement with—we contribute not only to our ongoing invisibilization, but also to a diminishment of academic culture and the debates pertinent to scholarly communication and knowledge production in general. (Sloniowski 2016)

Sloniowski (2016) describes where she sees the root cause of the perceptions by others:

> Like faculty, librarians are engaged in helping educate students by offering research help, as well as instruction in information literacy and research competencies. Although the term information literacy is not well-known outside of librarianship and librarians' work in this area is underrecognized, the skills required to find, organize, synthesize, and manipulate information are prized in the neoliberal knowledge economy, as information is the preeminent com-

modity form of contemporary capitalism (Eisenhower & Smith, 2010, p. 308). Academic librarians also maintain collections and organize information. We participate in gift economies through facilitating the borrowing of books and other items, as well as through our professional engagements with the open-access and open-data movements in scholarly publishing. We curate and maintain common spaces within which faculty and students may read and study, and, finally, along with our archivist colleagues, we engage in all matter of cultural stewardship and preservation activities in our collections, both physical and digital. In short, we operate as shadow labor whose role serves to reproduce the academy (Shirazi, 2014). The emphasis in our work, however, and how it is perceived by the public, is largely on the service side of our role rather than on the intellectual work involved in negotiating, evaluating, and manipulating scholarly information and its affects (as discussed at length in Harris and Chang 1988).

VOCATIONAL AWE

In a January 2018 article for *In the Library with the Lead Pipe*, Fobazi Ettarh describes the cornerstone of our profession: service. She relates it to democracy, quoting Hillary Clinton's statement from the 2017 ALA annual conference in Chicago: "You are guardians of the First Amendment and the freedom to read and to speak. The work you do is at the heart of an open, inclusive, diverse society [and] I believe that libraries and democracy go hand in hand" (Ettarh 2018). Then Ettarh (2018) asks how this statement helps us: "[W]hen the rhetoric surrounding librarianship borders on vocational and sacred language rather than acknowledging that librarianship is a profession or a discipline, and as an institution, historically and contemporarily flawed, we do ourselves a disservice." Her definition of *vocational awe* is the "set of ideas, values, and assumptions librarians have about themselves and the profession that result in beliefs that libraries as institutions are inherently good and sacred, and therefore beyond critique" (Ettarh 2018). Indeed, even the earliest books written about the profession indicate that the "very heart of librarianship is service to people" (Cowley 1928). Ettarh's goal in dismantling these mythologies surrounding libraries and librarians is to "deconstruct some of the assumptions and values so integrally woven into the field that supports and advocates for the people who work in libraries as much as it does for physical buildings and resources" (Ettarh 2018).

We can understand using *vocation* to describe our profession when we note that the first librarians were usually priests, "chiefly because the first writings of the race were concerned with law or with the problem of eternity, and the priests were both the law givers and the link between this world and the next. They were, moreover, the world's only educated men. They alone knew how to read and write the crude cuneiform scripts which were the race's first means of written communication" (Cowley 1928). To continue that line of thought, Ettarh (2018) describes the early physical spaces as sanctuary, shelter, and places of refuge and notes how today we continue to operate as "sanctuaries in the extended definition as a place of safety." Indeed, there is a clear divide between those who consider libraries to be places of safety for all and to express neutrality and those who do not. For example, a 2018 *American Libraries* article describes the 2018 midwinter ALA meeting and exhibits in Denver, where President Jim Neal's program provided a commentary on libraries as neutral organizations and librarianship as a neutral profession. That debate continues and plays into Ettarh's plea that we must replace the idea of vocational awe if we want to see more acceptance of librarianship as a profession.

RACE AND GENDER

Another angle for consideration of academic librarianship as a profession is discussion of race and gender. Lester Asheim points out in his 1978 review of where librarians stand as professionals that there is a social factor involved with the acceptance of librarians as true professionals: gender. He notes that the dominance of women in the field held down salaries and social status and that in a society that "jumps to a foregone conclusion about women's role," any occupation with a high proportion of women will automatically be depressed as a status (Asheim 1978).

Currently, more evidence of the roles of race and gender in our profession can be found in the growing numbers of books and articles that are "writing women back into" our history. Most notably, the ALA's vote in 2019 to strip Melvil Dewey's name from one of the association's highest honors, the Melvil Dewey Medal, shows a commitment to these efforts. Citing a history of racism, anti-Semitism, and sexual harassment, the ALA Council approved the measure after a resolution was successfully advanced at the ALA membership meeting during the 2019 ALA annual conference in Washington, DC. An article by Erin Blakemore on August 22, 2018, for History notes, "Dewey knew the modern libraries he needed would require cheap, eager labor—and the generation's few professional women, who were determined to prove themselves in a male-dominated world, were the perfect fit."

A 2016 article by Gina Schlesselman-Tarango describes both race and gender: "White supremacy and patriarchy have acted upon and through the white female body, which has implications for library and information science (LIS), a white- and female-dominated field." Through the archetype of Lady Bountiful, she writes about the "white female subject" in hopes of exposing her so that she can be banished from the field. In her literature review, she notes that discussions of Whiteness are limited, and others have noted that despite discussions of race in the literature and within the profession, the needle hasn't moved very far on increasing diversity within. For example, she notes that April Hathcock (2015) writes about the failure of diversity initiatives in library and information studies; Todd Honma (2005) discusses the epistemological forms of racism that exist in LIS; and Lisa Hussey (2010) approaches diversity from the rhetoric to describe the process and intended outcomes, where the question "Why are we lagging with diversity?" becomes "What are we trying to achieve?" Schlesselman-Tarango suggests that continuing to track the archetype, noting where it is most prevalent, and challenging it in the classroom are just a few ways that we can begin to build resistance and reshape the narrative to one that is more inclusionary.

By the early '90s, focus on our profession turned to technology and how it was beginning to disrupt everything. The literature review indicates that attention was turning from whether we were professionals to our "status." Chapter 2 reviews the prolific assortment of books, articles, and opinion pieces on the status of academic librarians in more depth. To conclude this discussion on the profession of academic librarianship, two quotes are offered here:

> Academic librarianship is an academic service business—not a bibliographic factory. Because we deal with the entire universe, our work tends to be messy, our procedures rarely algorithmic. Because we cater to human creativity, demand is variable and unpredictable, our work difficult or impossible to schedule systematically . . . intangible mental work that must be done by educated people who hold unique responsibilities for program, leadership, and teaching and who, like faculty, exercise an exclusive locus of power. (Veaner 1994)

> Academic libraries, from large research libraries to smaller college libraries, are products of the Enlightenment and its promotion of reason and freedom. The pursuit of knowledge for its own sake wherever it might lead, the examination of every possible topic in the light of reason, and the freedom to publish that research to the world—the underlying principles of modern universities—led to the inevitable creation of the libraries capable of supporting those goals. While scholars investigated, examined, experimented and wrote and wrote and wrote, academic librarians worked to acquire, preserve, organize, and make accessible the materials they needed, and in the process built up a national network of cooperative collections and services in the support of scholarship. (Bivens-Tatum 2011, 91)

Despite where one stands on the spectrum of "librarianship as a profession," the reality is that technology has challenged and deconstructed society's view of most professions. In her essay for *Creating the Future*, Barbara I. Dewey (1996) includes a quote from a 1995 *Forbes* article by Phillip E. Ross: "Think twice before investing years of your life developing your skills in law, medicine, accounting, travel agency, financial planning, insurance sales or library science. All these professions are beginning to face serious competition from computer programs." Sure enough, today we can see where technology has had a hand in raising questions of relevance for all these noted professions and then some.

CONCLUSION

Putting aside the questions and issues related to higher education, access to education, and the growing divide between "us and them," there are two key components in the definition of *professional* that appear to be missing: standard exams and consistent expectations for all. These questions related to the MLS, library school education, exams, and standards are discussed in later chapters. For now, one thing remains certain:

> Librarians cannot become complacent about the profession, their role in society, or their continuing opportunity to work in a relevant and meaningful occupation. . . . Changes are being forced upon both educational institutions and society in general by information technology. Librarians must step forward as leaders in setting information technology policies at the local, regional, and national level. Librarians who desire to lead, and thus ensure the health of the profession, must be activists, must collaborate with other information professionals, must become information technology experts, must continue to promote the importance of teaching, and must embrace their function as role-model. Regardless of the changes to come, librarians must be willing to act with flexibility and grace to play the roles outlined above. (Dewey 1996)

We cannot remain complacent.

Chapter Two

The Question of Status

"The librarian's office should rank with that of professor. . . . The profession of librarian should be distinctly recognized. Men and women should be encouraged to enter it, should be trained to discharge its duties, and should be rewarded, promoted, and honored in proportion to the services they render."—President Daniel Coit Gilman, Johns Hopkins University (1891)

The debate around faculty status and tenure for academic librarians now crosses more than a century. In 1884, amid fears that educators could be released simply due to the "capricious actions of boards of education and autocratic administrators" (Massman 1972), the National Education Association called for legal protection against arbitrary dismissal. In 1915, the Committee on Academic Freedom and Academic Tenure of the American Association of University Professors (AAUP) formulated its first statement on academic freedom and tenure called the "1915 Declaration of Principles." Officially approved by the association and its members at the December 31, 1915, annual meeting, the principles were refined over time and became the "1940 Statement on Principles of Academic Freedom and Tenure." The American Library Association (ALA) adapted the statement to fit libraries and on June 21, 1946, adopted "A Statement of Principles of Intellectual Freedom and Tenure for Librarians" (Massman 1972).

There continues to be support *for* faculty status at the national level. In 1973, the AAUP (2012) issued a "Joint Statement on Faculty Status of College and University Librarians." The statement was created together with the Association of College and Research Libraries (ACRL). It was reviewed again by both groups, revised to include language acknowledging technology in the libraries, and approved with the same level of support in 2013. Despite the adoption and endorsement, the struggle continues to be real, as there are some who propose that the support is ahistorical and unsound.

Considering that academic librarianship is a comparatively young profession, the fact that we remain misunderstood is not very surprising, especially when one stops to think about how academic libraries were formed in the nineteenth century. It was the increasingly centralized role of the library in higher education that led to the need for trained librarians and thus a proposal that we be considered like faculty. Robert B. Downs wrote a retrospective on the status of academic librarians in 1968 that surveys those early beginnings. He notes that his examination of annual catalogs of universities in the United States from 1870 to 1871 revealed librarians were listed variously as "Officers of Instruction and Government," with no academic title; "'Librarian' under a special heading after 'Faculty of the University'"; "College Officers"; or "Members of Faculties and Other Officers," or they weren't mentioned at all. The only universities who gave their chief librarians academic titles were those in which the chief librarian was already a member of the teaching faculty (Downs 1968).

Downs (1968) also notes that by the beginning of the twentieth century, some advances in the status of academic librarians could be found, and he credits that change to an 1876 US Bureau of Education special report titled *Public Libraries in the United States of America*. That report includes a proposal to create

> "professorships of books and reading," to guide students through the mazes of what, even then, was regarded as a bibliographical explosion. The instruction recommended would be primarily for the acquisition of knowledge, "the scientific use of books," i.e., sound methodology, and for "literary production." A chair of books and reading, it was suggested, might be filled by "an accomplished librarian." (Downs 1968)

He also notes that this recommendation was made during a time when the first library school was more than a decade in the making. Professional education for librarianship in America really began in 1887, when Melvil Dewey, chief librarian of Columbia College (later Columbia University), founded the School of Library Economy (Biggs 1981). Dr. Downs (1968) indicates that the Columbia University trustees ruled in 1911 that the "librarian shall have the rank of professor, the assistant librarian that of associate professor and the supervisors shall rank as assistant professors and bibliographers as instructors."

The first full exploration of the status of librarians in the twentieth century was undertaken by George A. Works (1927) in *College and University Problems*. In chapter 5, Works writes about the status of professional staff in college and university libraries. His study found that by the 1920s, college and university libraries had responsibilities to (1) facilitate and encourage research, (2) facilitate the work of teacher and student, and (3) offer opportunities for "cultural" reading by students and faculty (Works 1927).

A review of academic librarianship literature makes clear that perceptions and stereotypes play a role in the questions that swirl around faculty status for librarians. But just what is at stake here, and what are we talking about when we say "status"? For some, the word is used to describe exactly that—a level of assumed respect, competence, and standing. For example, Jane Forgotson (1961) writes that status is the "position an individual occupies with relation to a social group or organization. Each status carries with it a set of rights and duties, or a role to be performed. Status, then, represents the relative value assigned by the group to the role, and hence the rewards to be given for the performance of the role." For others, the status relates to benefits afforded certain groups. At stake for that group are benefits afforded most often to tenure-track academic faculty: higher salaries, sabbaticals, retirement benefits, vacation time, funding and support for professional activities, and the stability of tenure (see Massman 1972). With the AAUP's statement in support of faculty status for librarians in 1973 and the passing of the ACRL's *Standards for Academic Librarians* in 1972, one could ask why we are still debating the issue decades later?

The misconceptions of our early years may have played a role. Many authors note that while the growth of both volumes of books and the size of the student body had a positive impact on the addition of staff, there was also a link to public misperceptions. For many academic libraries, the administration's response to requests for more help resulted in what Works (1927) calls the "placing in library positions of persons who have grown old in the service of the university." In other words, administrators had no real understanding of the kind of work being done and would often "give to" the library unqualified staff. In other cases, professors were prone to stereotyping librarians as people who emphasize "orderliness, conformity, passivity, and unsociability" (Douglass 1957). Others note that from about 1876 through the first two decades of this century, standard indexes to library literature indicate to the casual observer that the love of books was a standard prerequisite for librarians. Mary Biggs identifies such actual titles as "Librarians' Pastime Reading" (1896); "Love of Books as a Basis for Librarianship" (1907); "Books That Have Influenced Me: A Symposium by Librarians" (1935); and "Do We Read in Our Profession?" (1940). She also notes that this began to change in the 1940s and 1950s, as

> articles indexed in Library Literature under the subject heading "Librarians' Reading" tended to deal exclusively with professional reading, and by the late 1970s even that concern seemed to have faded. From 1976 through 1978, only three articles appeared under the heading: one dealt with professional reading only, and the other two were published in Eastern European journals. (Biggs 1981)

Mary Biggs writes in "Sources of Tension and Conflict between Librarians and Faculty" that one response to the increasingly complex management of growing academic libraries was to appoint a faculty member as director and then bring in a librarian as his assistant. This pattern of what Biggs calls "scholar-librarian and librarian-assistant" instilled contempt in librarians, as it led to a pattern of creating prestigious positions for well-paid library directors, who then had their very underpaid and unappreciated assistants do most of the day-to-day work. It also tended to create assumptions about the educational differences between the two. However, Biggs notes, the system created a connection with the faculty who felt that their needs were comprehensible and important to those running the library. She continues, "Present day advocacy of 'subject specialists' and 'second master's degrees' implicitly recognizes the problem of a library staff without knowledge of, and respect for, books and methods of scholarly investigation" (Biggs 1981).

C. C. Williamson, in his *Training for Library Service* (1923), outlines the issues clouding the status question: administrators who don't take the time to identify the right qualifications for the different types of work in the library; library schools and their education programs for professional librarians (which are discussed more in a later chapter); and the importance of proper training for clerical workers—citing the need for both advanced academic degrees for professional librarians and certification programs for clerical staff.

Works (1927) lists the significant elements in defining the status of library staff as salary, retirement options, vacation time, tenure, relationship to faculty, and governance related to professional meeting attendance. The data he collected indicates great variety in status. Some institutions included all members of the library staff except the chief librarian in the clerical group; others gave a faculty rank commensurate with their salary; and many "provisions" indicate partial recognition of the need for higher levels or professional status. He notes that many of these issues just need to be talked through with university and college leaders, as all the rapid changes and growth happened to fill important gaps; gone were the days where the institution had need only for a library with one librarian and a handful of untrained help (Works 1927).

A 1924 report from the College and Reference Section of the ALA's committee titled *Educational Qualifications and Status of the Professional Librarian in Colleges and Universities* proposes that appropriate rank; salary; and privileges (such as vacation, pension allowance, and membership on boards and committees) should be the factors to determine the professional members of the library staff. The report also suggests that "in the responsibilities that must be carried in the large university, the position of librarian is fairly comparable with the position of dean. In the smaller institution it perhaps is more fairly compared with the directorship of a school or the headship of a department."

Between the late 1920s and early 1960s, the literature related to the status of academic librarians proliferated (see, for example, Kirkpatrick 1947, Lundy 1951, Maloy 1939, and McAnally 1957). By 1964, academic status for librarians had become firmly established in a "considerable number" of American universities (Downs 1968). Arthur McAnally (1957) notes that of

> ninety-seven replies received, the status held by professional librarians, in descending order of frequency, was: academic status, thirty; faculty status, twenty-four; professional, administrative, and special, twenty-three; non-academic and uncertain, twelve; mixed, six; and state civil service, two. Academic or faculty status was held by fifty-four of the ninety-seven library staffs. Requests for academic or faculty status had been disapproved in twenty-three institutions, four times in one particular university.

He defines *faculty status* as the

> possession of all or most of the privileges of the classroom teaching faculty, including faculty rank. Academic status is held to be the possession of some but not all usual faculty privileges, with definite classification as academic but always without faculty rank. Academic status thus may be considered a kind of reduced faculty status. Because faculty status and academic status are quite similar, and for convenience, the term academic status is used loosely throughout the rest of this paper to apply to both forms. (McAnally 1957)

He also notes that the decision about whether to approve a request for academic status was affected by a variety of factors, which he categorized into six groups: (1) institutional, (2) administrative and financial, (3) pertaining to the faculty, (4) originating in the library, (5) other intrainstitutional forces, and (6) extrainstitutional forces. Institutional factors were related to "influence" or "character" of the institution:

> Almost three-fourths of the separate land-grant institutions (often called agricultural and mechanical colleges until recently) grant academic status to their professional librarians. Two-thirds of the state universities which are also the land-grant institutions for their state have granted academic status, as have two-thirds of the technical institutes. State universities and private universities bring up the rear, with slightly less than half of both granting academic status to their librarians. (McAnally 1957)

Among administrative factors, he notes that a "library-minded" president of the university and his chief assistants were most important. Regarding library conditions, he notes that the library should be conducting individual teaching and counseling, bibliographical, and other research; that it should be working actively to promote independent and cultural learning; and that the library staff ought to be "professionally alert and intellectually alive" (McAnally 1957).

In 1981, an ACRL "Academic Status Survey" indicated that 44 percent of 126 libraries polled claimed to have full faculty rank, status, and privileges for their librarians. Areas with the greatest discrepancy between librarians and teaching faculty involve vacations (40 percent say was not equivalent), salaries (37 percent), tenure (33 percent), and sabbaticals (30 percent). The literature review notes that the term *faculty status* typically designates faculty ranks (titles); academic year appointments; release time for research and professional activities; academic freedom (in early days, this usually applied to book selection; more often today this refers to freedom of academic expression); access to institutional travel and research funds; equivalent vacations and pay scales; eligibility for faculty governance work; sabbaticals and tenure; and evaluation by identical criteria used for faculty or similar criteria modified to reflect actual job content (DeBoer and Culotta 1987).

In addition to these more tangible benefits of seeking faculty status, another is its symbolic, psychological significance. A recurring theme throughout the research indicates that the original purpose was "historically to acknowledge the important role academic librarians play in successful research, teaching, and learning" (Leonhardt 2004).

In 1971, the ACRL established "Standards for Faculty Status for College and University Librarians." They were revised in 1992 and again in 2001. Those standards are as follows:

- Librarians perform professional responsibilities.
- Librarians have an academic form of governance for the library faculty.
- Librarians have equal representation in all college or university governance.
- Librarians receive compensation comparable to that of other faculty.
- Librarians are covered by tenure policies.
- Librarians are promoted in rank based on a peer review system.
- Librarians are eligible for sabbatical and other leaves.
- Librarians have access to research and professional development funds.
- Librarians have the same academic freedom protections as other faculty.

Using the standards as a framework, Danielle Bodrero Hoggan wrote an article for *portal: Libraries and the Academy* outlining the advantages and disadvantages of faculty status for academic librarians. Among the advantages of faculty status, are higher stature and recognition within the university, better relationships with other campus faculty, more responsiveness to change and innovation, higher salaries, continuous appointment, professional development, representation in faculty governance, leave options, job satisfaction, teaching goals, and publication quantity and quality (Hoggan 2003).

Under disadvantages, Hoggan notes that librarians with faculty status experience more pressure to do research, publish, and attend meetings, which detracts from time spent on more traditional librarianship duties. In addition, some library faculty experience resentment from other faculty members; added stress; a tendency toward quantity over quality in publication; negative lifestyle impact; and "nominal faculty status," which is the title without all of the accompanying privileges (Hoggan 2003).

While the majority of the research indicates support for faculty status for academic librarians, there are also those who question the validity of both the terminal degree and faculty status. Phillip J. Jones, W. Bede Mitchell, and Jean A. Major (1998) examine more than a half-century of library literature to defend their argument that the ACRL statement created in 1975 that "enshrined the American Library Association–accredited master's degree in library science (ALA-MLS) as the terminal degree for academic librarianship" has had a "chilling effect on any sustained, critical debate on this topic." The "Statement on the Terminal Professional Degree for Academic Librarians" states, "The master's degree from a program accredited by the American Library Association or from a program in a country with a formal accreditation process as identified by ALA's Human Resource Development and Recruitment Office is the appropriate terminal professional degree for academic librarians" (ACRL 2011). It was first approved as policy by the board of directors of the ACRL, a division of the ALA, on January 23, 1975, then reviewed and reaffirmed in 2001, 2007, 2011, and 2018.

Jones, Mitchell, and Major (1998) consider the issue of faculty status for academic librarians "controversial" and believe the ACRL statement has managed to sustain debate on both sides of the issue. The authors note that shortly after the 1975 statement on the terminal degree, "debate flared," and the topic was on center stage during a symposium examining the "identity" of academic librarianship, where three of seven authors "disagreed with ACRL's recent position" (Jones, Mitchell, and Major 1998). Post-1975, after a thorough review of the literature, the authors note that the debate "largely faded," a shift they say "testifies to the 'success' of the ACRL statement to inhibit debate" (Jones, Mitchell, and Major 1998).

The root of the debate for Jones, Mitchell, and Major is answering the question "What is the terminal degree?":

> Examining library literature after 1975 may lead one to surmise the ALA-MLS. But to one who peruses earlier texts on the topic, reads between the lines of latter ones, and looks at professional practice, the ahistoricity of the ALA-MLS as the absolute, sole terminal degree for academic librarianship becomes patent. The 1975 terminal degree statement stands on shaky ground. . . . Academic librarianship is a vast vocation with numerous positions requiring varying skills, experiences, and educations, to which current position advertisements attest. Ultimately the profession may determine that the terminal

degree may be an outmoded concept unsuited to academic library preparation in the 21st century. Consequently, the flexible passage on academic preparation in the 1959 Standards may serve as the ideal template for future debate and professional practice. It is time for academic librarians to meet the role of academic graduate work in their profession. (Jones, Mitchell, and Major 1998)

Their argument is that we "ought to have more graduate degrees, both at the doctoral and master's level, represented on our staff, in subject fields, as well as in library science" and that by focusing only on one degree (the MLS), we ignore other, also acceptable graduate work (Jones, Mitchell, and Major 1998). In addition, these authors note that the 1975 terminal degree statement ended the discussion of considering the PhD as the more appropriate terminal degree for academic librarians and faculty status.

In 1993, Charles Lowry conducted a study on the employment status of librarians, where he collected data from two groups of academic libraries in higher education—a random sample of all institutions in the United States and all academic members of the Association of Research Libraries. This data provided a twenty-year retrospective of librarians' status and indicated that 67 percent of higher education institutions granted faculty status. This data also indicated that faculty status for librarians had expanded greatly, although Lowry notes that the process had slowed over the same time period. From 1975 through the 1990s, we can see that most academic librarians could assume that positions would include faculty status and, in many cases, tenure. Beginning with the turn of the century, however, that all began to change.

In 2016, William H. Walters wrote about the faculty status of librarians at US research universities,

> exploring the relationships among the various components of faculty status, first by presenting key findings from 30 studies that have evaluated the prevalence of faculty status in American colleges and universities, then by reporting on a faculty status survey completed by the library directors at 124 U.S. research universities. The survey data are used to clarify the relationships among 12 components of faculty status: nominal faculty status, tenure, professor ranks, peer review, scholarship, faculty senate, other committees, sabbaticals, flexible work, nine-month year, research funds, and equivalent salaries.

His work notes "several hundred" papers written about academic librarians and faculty status over several decades, most of those dealing with themes of prevalence, the various components, arguments for and against, differences between the faculty role and the librarian role, standards, impact, and implications for managers. He found the discussions to be "nebulous" and that

> any one component of faculty status, such as eligibility for tenure, eligibility for sabbaticals, or the use of peer review in promotion decisions, is likely to be

found at only some of the institutions that grant faculty status to librarians. As a result, studies of faculty status—case studies, in particular—often report findings that are not directly comparable with those of prior investigations. (Walters 2016)

Walters's paper also includes the results of his August 2015 online survey of library directors (deans or university librarians) from research universities. The survey group included the 202 institutions ranked in the 2015 "National Universities" category of *US News and World Report*, plus the one ARL university not included in that group. Of the survey requests sent via e-mail invitation, 124 responses were collected (61 percent response rate), and Walters's review of the data suggest some interesting findings. Librarians are "least likely to have faculty status at the elite, private research universities" (confirming previous reports that faculty status is especially common among librarians at public rather than private universities) and "just 3 of the 18 private ARL universities in the sample grant faculty status to librarians" (Walters 2016). Additionally, he notes that the findings describe "recent changes in the prevalence of faculty status (and its various components)"; confirms that "faculty status is more common at public (rather than private) institutions and less common at universities near the top of the U.S. News rankings"; offers some helpful points of comparison for future studies regarding the specific components of faculty status; provides updates to work completed between 2008 and 2015; and points out the difficulty of responding to "yes-or-no" questions (Walters 2016).

With noted difficulties in tracking academic libraries that change the status of their librarians over time, do we know whether one institution changed its status for librarians? If so, why, and how do we find out about them? In the last decade, there have been reports of several colleges and universities changing course. The University of Virginia was one of the first to make a change in status for their librarians (see Dunn 2013 and Horowitz 2013), and Walters notes that according to his survey responses, Iowa State University and South Dakota State University implemented new policies that indicate librarians were hired prior to 2012–2013 with faculty status and post-2013 without (Walters 2016). Why does this happen?

In her *Chronicle of Higher Education* article, Sydni Dunn (2013) writes that librarians "on many campuses have long been considered faculty, but some institutions are now reclassifying the position as a staff job as they reassess the role of their research libraries more broadly." Dunn (2013) notes that East Carolina University was, at the same time,

> weighing a plan that may strip its future librarians of faculty status, their ability to earn tenure, or both. Debates on those campuses follow similar changes enacted elsewhere in recent years. The Alamo Community College District, in San Antonio, dropped faculty rank for its librarians in 2011. That

same year, Mt. Hood Community College, in Gresham, Ore., laid off its full-time faculty librarians and replaced them with library staff.

What does faculty status look like for academic librarians today, and what does it mean for current LIS graduates? An October 2020 study by Karen Antell and Susan Hahn titled "Faculty Status: The Next Generation Employment Status Preferences among Millennial LIS Students and New Librarians at ARL Institutions" finds that the "themes that emerge from the results indicate that job security is an especially strong concern for this population of academic librarians and students, that faculty status and the opportunity to earn tenure are associated with perceived job security, and that this population views academic librarians' work as being equal to that of 'regular' faculty members." Will this new evidence change anything? Without any formal standards or requirements to publicize tenure or faculty status information in job ads, it is hard to find. Some job ads include the information, but most do not. A 2018 blog intended as an "aid to Rank and Tenure committees, library administrators, librarian job applicants, and others interested in issues related to professional status in the library science field" notes that there are five versions of library faculty status identified by academic libraries. The site's author, Chris Lewis (2018), writes that the chief goal of the site is to "simplify the process of finding an institution comparable to one's own in regard to the professional status of its librarians." In addition, the site offers a good guide to identify, at a moment in time, the status of academic librarians. The five categories are as follows:

1. Librarians with full faculty status and tenure, which includes librarians with titles denoting their rank (e.g., associate professor or associate librarian), who are likely required to publish, have seats on faculty committees, and are considered members of the university's faculty with accompanying benefits (164, or approximately 59 percent of institutions).
2. Librarians with faculty or academic status but no tenure whose librarians likely have titles denoting their rank, have the option to contribute to the profession but may not be required to, may have seats on faculty committees, and have renewable contracts with opportunities for continuing appointments (52, or approximately 19 percent of institutions).
3. Librarians with a mix of professional statuses in these institutions have tenure-track and non-tenure-track librarians or faculty and nonfaculty librarians or a combination of each (20, or approximately 7 percent of institutions).
4. Librarians without faculty or academic status, who have staff positions without the protections or privileges accorded to faculty or librarians with academic status (27, or approximately 10 percent of institutions).

5. Librarians without faculty or academic status but with status similar to tenure. These librarians may have formal ranks, may have an option to contribute to the profession but are not required to, do not serve on faculty committees or receive other faculty benefits, have renewable contracts with opportunities for continuing appointments (17, or approximately 6 percent of institutions).

What the blog doesn't capture are changes in the status of their academic librarians—and why. It has the potential, though, to become a great resource for documenting the status and changes for all academic libraries.

CONCLUSION

What does all this information mean for academic librarians today? For one, we can see that the debate for and against faculty status is still active. Some believing that the ACRL's standards have deprived the profession of stronger support for the PhD as the terminal degree in line with the rest of academe, while others believe that the MLS saves us from having to compare ourselves to a more formal system.

We have come no closer to a resolution than Carl Hintz surmised in 1968 when he indicated that the "exact definition of academic status remains uncertain." And this should be troubling to us as a profession. What are the anchors that will help us answer these questions once and for all? In scholarship and contribution? In education? The next chapter looks closer at scholarship and contribution.

Chapter Three

Anchoring the Profession in Scholarship

"If librarianship is to develop as the times demand or opportunity offers, it too must be firmly undergirded with the results of basic and continuing research. Some of it, at least, must be anticipatory. Research which answers questions already posed is valuable, that which creates and proposes is invaluable. Research produces knowledge. Knowledge is needed for understanding. Understanding, combined with skill leads to effective action."—Lowell Martin

PREFACE TO 1957 *LIBRARY TRENDS* ISSUE
ON RESEARCH IN LIBRARIANSHIP

Of the three main tenets identifying academic librarianship, the production of scholarship, or requirement to publish, is a central component, particularly for those required to go through the promotion and tenure process. And yet, this essential piece is one of the least explored issues of our profession. There remains much scrutiny, criticism, and challenge of the notion that academic librarians are, fundamentally, researchers. By many accounts, academic librarians conducting research was considered to have "limited value." This chapter explores research conducted by academic librarians, looks back to how and where definitions were formed, examines whether there were widely recognized and established guidelines or standards, and determines impact.

According to an article by Gay Helen Perkins and Amy Slowik in 2013, the "early history of research in academic libraries suggested a limited value for library practitioners, a conclusion that Wallace at the University of Oklahoma articulated in 2007. Since the 1850s, librarianship has been a professional practice with research efforts, professional groups, conferences, practice-oriented publications, and best practices." They note that it was thanks to two events in the early 1900s that brought a new focus to research for librarians: "In 1921, scientific methodology for library and information science research emerged from the Graduate Library School at the University of Chicago. The first American Library Association division, the ACRL or the Association of College and Reference Libraries, started in 1940" (Perkins and Slowik 2013). The ACRL would begin to set standards and define guidelines for academic status; the terminal degree; certification; professional development; the appointment, promotion, and tenure process; and faculty status (see ACRL Board of Directors 2011; ACRL Committee on the Status of Academic Librarians 2007; and ACRL Research Planning and Review Committee 2020 for exact language). It does not appear, however, to have defined research. Perkins and Slowik (2013) note that while there would be publications between 1960 and 1980, few of them addressed the questions related to research in the profession. They reference articles on publication outputs (deSimone Watson 1977), support for publishing and research activities (Bridegam 1978; Rayman and Goudy 1980), and standards related to librarian status (Davey and Andrews 1978).

RESEARCH IN LIBRARY AND INFORMATION SCIENCE

There is one publication that addresses the question of research in the early literature: a *Library Trends* issue published in 1957 on research in librarianship. The authors note that prior to the 1950s there was a hit-or-miss approach to research within our profession, but there was a developing interest during the 1950s in activity and research in librarianship. Lancour (1957) writes, "Doctoral programs have been set up in at least six library schools and more are under consideration. The recent shift to the master's level of professional training, despite the fact that many schools do not have an essay requirement, nevertheless has greatly increased the number of master's essays written each year over the number produced prior to 1951." He notes that during the same time, financial support for research greatly increased, with grants provided in part for research, established by the Council on Library Resources and others, such as the Carnegie Corporation, Rockefeller Foundation, United States Steel Foundation, Remington Rand, and the Lilly Endowment, allowing for expenditures into research.

In the introduction of that same issue, Maurice Tauber, professor in the School of Library Service at Columbia University, outlines the issues related to the scarcity of research: improper training by library schools in research methods, little time for those in practicing roles for original studies, and "meager" financial support of library investigations. He notes that part of the problem lay in the perceptions of practicing librarians, particularly those who believe that librarianship is an art, "not subject to the exact measurements of scientific inquiry or objective study" (Tauber 1957). Tauber (1957) responds that libraries have become complex organizations and that "careful studies of problems arising out of the complexity should provide the librarian with a greater understanding, should improve his judgment, and should reduce the load of his work. Research will never replace the art in librarianship; it may, however, make the practice of such art easier, and more effective."

Tauber (1957) outlines the content of the rest of the *Library Trends* issue:

- Successful library research recognizes the "importance of social, cultural, and other influences upon the library."
- Opportunities for research lay in the philosophy of librarianship and how libraries relate to government and society, their relationship with mass communication, their problems of communication, the "untouched field of human relations," and the "quality and effectiveness of service to individuals."
- Exploring all phases of resources for operations and services is essential.
- Standards for descriptive cataloging, subject cataloging, and classification on national and international bases must be developed as records "become more complex with growing collections."
- "[I]nvestigation into ways and means of content analysis, storage of information, and immediate retrieval has been accelerated."
- "[A]ll aspects of library education—programs, curricula, instructional methods, relations between performance on the job and library school training, and the place of the library school in the structure of higher education"—must be examined.
- Library research must recognize the "rigid methodologies of other disciplines."
- "Coordinated support of research by professional associations in relation to the library schools and other agencies is essential."
- "Library school faculties, particularly those associated with institutions having advanced or doctoral programs, have a special responsibility for development of integrated programs of research."
- "Financial support is necessary" for library research.

In his conclusion, Tauber notes that research in librarianship should be reexamined periodically for continued development and successful applications of research methodologies.

In a 1989 issue of the *Library and Information Science Research: An International Journal*, Jeffrey Katzer's editorial describes the American Library Association (ALA) and the status of LIS research. He notes that over fifty years, there has been progress in how well our research studies were conceived and conducted. Unfortunately, he says, there is still a way to go, and he offers three major causes for the state of our research:

1. Too much of what has been called research falls under the heading of consulting or demonstration projects.
2. Too few of our academic and professional colleagues have the inclination or training needed for research.
3. Not enough resources are available to support research on anything more than an opportunistic basis.

Katzer says that the influence of the ALA was "detrimental" to research; it's too large, with influence that is too broad to be helpful. In addition, he notes that the ALA's mission statement, priorities, and goals do not mention research. Interestingly, the Library Research Round Table (LRRT) was founded in 1968 to extend and improve library research, to provide public program opportunities for describing and evaluating library research projects and disseminating their findings, to inform and educate ALA members about research techniques and their usefulness in obtaining information with which to reach administrative decisions and solve problems, and to expand the theoretical base of the field (ALA n.d.c.). It is clear from their website that information began appearing in 1988, so one has to wonder what impact this roundtable was able to make in the twenty previous years.

The First Congress on Professional Education (April 1999) recommended that the ALA "disseminate (in appropriate ways) the findings and conclusions from research and their implications for professional practice." Additionally, the ALA executive board asked the Committee on Research and Statistics to prepare "findings and recommendations related to the effective dissemination of research" (ALA 2001). After some investigation and discussion of how the ALA and similar associations disseminate research findings, the committee reflected on the several parties involved in the effective dissemination of research results in any practice discipline. It says,

> It is our belief that four major parties play a role: the researchers, the practitioners, the educators, and the professional associations.
>
> 1. The Researchers must keep in mind that unless the implications of research are communicated to practitioners, the results are of little value.
> 2. The Practitioners must keep in mind that systematic attention to these findings is a professional obligation.
> 3. The Educators must base course work on a diligent awareness of research findings and reflection on their implications.
> 4. The Professional Associations must disseminate results purposefully and encourage the development of communication among all those concerned. (ALA 2001)

We start to see more attention being paid again to "research" in the 1990s.

INCREASING RESEARCH STRATEGIES

In 1991, Charles McClure and Peter Hernon edited *Library and Information Science Research: Perspectives and Strategies for Improvement*. It was and continues to be the most comprehensive monograph devoted strictly to research within library and information science. In the first chapter, Peter Hernon notes that a theme of the book is "that we should not be satisfied with the status of library and information science as a profession" (Hernon 1991). He says that a "discipline only grows and thrives if its body of basic and applied research increases. Such research may sustain a discipline, provide a basis for the development of new fields of inquiry, and suggest approaches for studying problems" (Hernon 1991). The definition of *research* Hernon (1991) offers is "any conscious premeditated inquiry—any investigation which seeks to increase one's knowledge of a situation." Then, wanting to offer a more focused definition to cover the types of research in LIS, he defines *parameters* as

- discovery or creation of knowledge or theory building;
- testing, confirmation, revision, and refutation of knowledge and theory; and/or
- investigation of a problem for local decision making.

The inquiry process, Hernon notes, has five activities:

1. Reflective inquiry (identification of a problem, conducting a literature search to place the problem in proper perspective, and formulation of a logical or theoretical framework, objectives, and hypotheses/research questions)
2. Adoption of appropriate procedures (research design and methodologies)
3. Collection of data
4. Data analysis
5. Presentation of findings and recommendations for future study

In conclusion, Hernon (1991) says that the future

> requires a commitment on the part of researchers and practitioners to accept LIS as a discipline and a profession, to better define the discipline of LIS, and to demonstrate that disciplinary base. . . . Research in LIS, or any profession for that matter, should encourage practitioners to ask why and not merely to do something. Greater attention to high quality basic and applied research focus-

ing on theory building and modeling provides a key link in the transition of LIS from a profession to a discipline.

In a follow-up article, Peter Hernon and Candy Schwartz (1993) note that research is "not an activity that occurs at the fringes of the field. Rather, it is central to the continued development of library and information science as a profession or discipline represented by graduate programs within academia."

In 2002, Ronald Powell, Lynda Baker, and Joseph Mika sent a questionnaire to members of the American Library Association, the American Society for Information Science and Technology, the Medical Library Association, and the Special Libraries Association. They found that many LIS practitioners were still not heavily involved in research. Of 1,444 questionnaires sent, they received 615 responses, and an analysis of those responses revealed that "90% of LIS practitioners in the United States and Canada regularly read at least one research journal, nearly 62% regularly read research-based articles, approximately 50% occasionally apply research results to professional practices, and 42% occasionally or frequently perform research related to their job or to the LIS profession" (Powell, Baker, and Mika 2002).

The results were disappointing. Four questions focused on conducting and publishing research. Of those who had conducted research, 83.7 percent indicated that they "had not published the results of their research" (Powell, Baker, and Mika 2002). The authors concluded that a "considerable number of practitioners regularly read research journals and articles, do research, apply the results of research, and engage in self-education as a means for learning about research methods—activities that indicate a positive attitude toward research" (Powell, Baker, and Mika 2002). And in response to the last question ("How do LIS practitioners assess their research skills?"), approximately 15 percent noted that they "did not have enough expertise in research methods" (Powell, Baker, and Mika 2002). Finally, the authors suggest that if research is to play an important role going forward, "then LIS professionals of all types, the agencies responsible for educating them, and their employing organizations must give more attention to this critical activity" (Powell, Baker, and Mika 2002). Considering that research and publication are central to the continued development of our profession, these results are a bit disconcerting.

More disconcerting news comes from Stephen Wiberley, Julie Hurd, and Ann Weller, who found declines in publication patterns of academic librarians. In several articles reviewing five-year time frames from 1993 to 2002, Wiberley, Hurd, and Weller (2006) found "across-the-board declines in the number and proportion of peer-reviewed articles written by academic librarians, as well as a decrease in the number of academic librarian authors as a whole"; specifically, the decline was close to 13 percent. As to the cause of the decline, they considered the "change in the number of refereed LIS journals; potential number of authors; impact of individual journals; and fluctuations in publication patterns" to be possible sources (Wiberley, Hurd, and Weller 2006). For comparison purposes, a 1985 article by Sylvia C. Krausse and Janice F. Sieburth reviews patterns of authorship in library journals and notes twelve library science journal contributions by academic librarians between 1973 and 1982, an increase from 28 to 42 percent.

S. Craig Finlay, Chaoqun Ni, Andrew Tsou, and Cassidy R. Sugimoto continued the investigation into publishing patterns with their 2013 *portal: Libraries and the Academy* article. They note that understanding publishing patterns is "crucial to an understanding of the discipline itself. Documenting authorship of scholarly literature within a field allows researchers to access 'sources of strength in research and scholarship and the field's pace among other disciplines'" (Finlay et al. 2013). They write that their study sought to answer questions regarding the stability of the proportion of librarian authors since 1955, the topics of LIS literature, and the frequency of citations of librarian and nonlibrarian authors (Finlay et al. 2013).

Finlay and colleagues note that the continued requirement to publish must include consideration of the struggles, like working with a twelve-month contract and forty-hour work week with various service requirements, which many authors assert creates an unsustainable model for continued success (see Brown 2001; Cosgriff, Kenney, and McMillan 1990; and Mitchell and Reichel 1999 for more on this topic). Shalu Gillum offers another perspective, as her research suggests that we need to seriously consider the decision by many universities to do away with tenure. Gillum (2010) finds that "without the lure of promotion and tenure, there is little motivation for librarians to contribute to the body of LIS literature." She cites a study conducted by Joseph Fennewald in 2008, which finds that the "research performed by librarians in their scholarly writing process actually helps them with their daily problem solving, which translates into better customer service" (Gillum 2010). Fennewald (2008) also notes that a recurring motivation for those academic librarians who published is a belief that the "importance of research is to identify new knowledge that will enhance practice."

RESEARCH MOTIVATIONS

Joseph Fennewald (2008) conducted his research to allow librarians to "describe in their own words what motivates them to conduct research; what programs, experiences, or support they have found useful; and what hindrances they have faced." He interviewed librarians at Pennsylvania State University, as previous studies of research productivity often placed Penn State within the top five institutions producing research in library and information sciences. Based on the responses from the twenty-five librarians he interviewed, Fennewald (2008) concludes that, in addition to expectations for conducting research as a requirement for promotion and tenure, many had a "commitment to add to the body of professional knowledge" and a "desire to enhance and expand services within the library, their intellectual curiosity, or a sense of satisfaction with the outcome of 'being published.'"

Indeed, many other advocates for a commitment to scholarly research and publication echo Fennewald, including that the role of the academic librarian continues to change and those changes make it even more important that we continue to produce research and scholarship. Finlay and colleagues (2013) come to the same conclusion, noting that a

> decline in librarian-authored research, coupled with significant differences in the topics of librarian-authored research suggests that the character of LIS literature is likely to change in the near future, if present decline in librarian-authored research continues. The apparent disengagement of librarians from the traditional channels of scholarly communication will necessarily decrease librarians' familiarity with scholarly communication, and this in turn may affect how librarians, especially those employed at academic institutions, interact with students and academics who are conducting research. . . . This would no doubt have important pedagogical implications for students and academics whose collective research interests infrequently extend to the very field they are seeking to enter.

In a 2017 study designed to follow up on these two studies to "see if the changes observed were indicative of long-term trends or just momentary variations," researchers Deborah D. Blecic, Stephen E. Wiberley Jr., Sandra L. De Groote, John Cullars, Mary Shultz, and Vivian Chan came to several interesting conclusions. Their thorough review not only looked at publication patterns but also included status, staffing size, and staffing patterns over the same years previously covered, 2003–2012. The authors (referenced in the article as the "study team") found that "[a]t all but one, some or all of the librarians had faculty status with tenure (FS&T). The exception offered a status similar to tenure" (Blecic et al. 2017). They note this as an important indicator for the future of the publishing activity in our professional literature (Blecic et al. 2017).

In addition, a 2006 study of academic librarians who hold subject doctorates in the United States and Canada assessed their basic characteristics, educational and career choices, and current positions. Thea Lindquist and Todd Gilman (2008) gathered data through an online survey and used that data "to describe and analyze their MLS-holding patterns, timing and motivation for educational and career choices, field of subject expertise, range of current positions, and projected retirement trends." Their results provide a great deal of information about the differences perceived by those holding PhDs. Most interestingly, when asked about the advantages of having the

PhD, respondents noted "credibility with teaching faculty" (36.1 percent), "subject expertise" (34.5 percent), "ability to relate to academic users" (26.7 percent), and an "in-depth understanding of the research process" (26.3 percent) (Gilman and Lindquist 2010). Notably missing was an opportunity to contribute new knowledge to the field. Also of interest, some respondents expanded on their areas of publication; 51 percent indicated that they publish most in LIS; 42.7 percent in the subject area in which they earned their doctorate; and 6.3 percent in another subject area (Gilman and Lindquist 2010). This information is more likely directly related to the findings of Finlay and colleagues in 2013.

In a follow-up study, S. Craig Finlay, Cassidy R. Sugimoto, Daifeng Li, and Terrell G. Russell reviewed LIS dissertation titles and abstracts. The results of that study found "general empirical support for long-held anecdotal assertions that libraries are no longer the primary research focus at the doctoral level in LIS" (Finlay et al. 2012). Their findings confirmed those earlier findings as well as a continued drop in contributions.

Because contribution to the profession is a hallmark of library faculty status and a requirement for rank, promotion, or tenure, this was disturbing. There are even more questions that we can ask, such as:

- What is produced?
- How do academic librarians conduct research?
- Where does it take place?
- Who produces the scholarship?
- What connections do they have to faculty in other disciplines?
- What areas for scholarship are missing, and how we can address those gaps?
- How is academic rigor which some say is lacking in our research, applied?

What we find from that research can and should determine some possible solutions.

DECLINE IN PUBLICATION

All the authors reviewed indicate that our number-one cause for concern should be this decline in the volume of publication by academic librarians. US academic librarians bring a unique perspective to LIS literature and a focus on library practice, often evidence-based. Indeed, an analysis of articles published in *College and Research Libraries* finds that collections, services, staffing, and the Internet are the top research topics. It also reveals that a wide variety of researchable questions remain to be studied and reported (Bao 2000).

Deborah D. Blecic and colleagues (2017) agree that the decline in academic librarians' overall publication rates deserve further investigation. In their May 2017 article "Publication Patterns of U.S. Academic Librarians and Libraries from 2003 to 2012," they review the studies by Wiberley, Hurd, and Weller (2006) and add some questions to their profile. For example, they examine the number of articles produced by each author, whether an increase in coauthorship played a role in declining overall numbers, whether an institution's inclusion of faculty status for librarians affected production, and whether declining staffing numbers had an impact.

Blecic and colleagues (2017) examined 1,698 issues published by 41 LIS journals between 2003 and 2012 and found a total of 10,575 refereed articles, of which one or more US academic librarians (USALs) authored 3,913 (37 percent). Overall, they found 3,870 USALs from 696 different libraries contributed at least one peer-reviewed article to the journals studied. Their data suggests that the overall contributions to journal literature came from a small percentage of USALs and libraries. In a comparison of the unique USAL names and number of unique institutions, they found 2,182 between 2003 and 2007 and 2,268 between 2008 and 2012. Further, they indicate that while "these two counts add up to 4,450, the number of unique USAL author names for the ten years is 3,870, indicating that 580 USAL authors (15%) published in both time periods. Most USAL authors published only once in ten years, 1,602 in 2003–2007 and 1,688 in 2008–2012" (Blecic et al. 2017). According to the National Center for Education Statistics report for fall 2012, "there were 26,606 librarians at 3,172 responding U.S. academic libraries (out of 3,793 U.S. academic libraries surveyed). These data indicate that less than 10 percent of USALs published a peer-reviewed journal article in one of the major LIS journals studied during a five-year period" (Blecic et al. 2017). Their results also "suggest that an increase in coauthorship rates resulted in more articles for individuals (author instances), but not more articles for the profession. Large, public, research-intensive universities had high-contributing libraries, but some experienced staffing decreases that impacted productivity" (Blecic et al. 2017).

Finally, Blecic and colleagues propose that the decline in academic librarians' overall publication rates deserve further investigation, such as whether an aging library workforce with more tenured librarians resulted in fewer untenured librarians with the most incentive to produce. They also wonder whether the elimination of some library schools at private research universities created a culture that was less encouraging for academic librarian scholarship. They looked at the construction of work assignments; the complexities of rapid change coupled with widespread budgetary pressures, resulting in less time for research; and the possibility that academic librarians are simply choosing to share their scholarship in other ways, such as via bibliographic essays, blogs, other social media outlets, book chapters, or different types of journals. Here again, we are faced with more questions than answers.

One thing all the authors agree on: The profession needs to notice the decrease in practitioners' contributions to the literature, investigate the factors that may be contributing to the situation, and see if any action can be taken to further support scholarly research. There is, however, one unexplored area of research that is investigated more fully here.

IMPACT OF THE NONLIBRARY RESEARCH AGENDA

As far back as 1981, there was another perspective on contribution to scholarship, and it became a growing trend that remains. It began with a recommendation that if academic librarians wanted to be seen as peers by teaching faculty, then they should spend their time contributing to a "nonlibrary" research agenda. Black and Leysen (1994) note that the "acceptability and significance of publications outside the field of librarianship is frequently debated." Since then, other authors have joined the debate, noting that benefits include that their "subject matter knowledge and research backgrounds can influence their work on the library's instructional projects, the content of their own instruction, their collaboration with faculty, and their mentorship of students, as well as their collection development practices" (Montelongo et al. 2010). Other authors with similar responses include Christiansen, Stombler, and Thaxton 2004; Floyd and Phillips 1997; and Jackson 2000.

One study on the value of research in academic libraries includes phone interviews with administrators in academic libraries. Those interviewees noted themes of library research they would like to see explored, including the effects of change in the library's mission, organization, and role; evidence-based research on user needs and academic study patterns; impact of the economy; impact of information literacy; library environment as study space; effects of Google mass digitization on technical services; and changes needed in library schools (Perkins and Slowik 2013). And yet, seven of those same interviewees indicated that they either had no publications or "had not published in the area of library sciences" (Perkins and Slowik 2013).

In 2014, Susan Thomas and Anne Leonard conducted a study of academic librarians' scholarship and creative work outside of LIS and their work in other professions. They articulate their reasoning to consider scholarship outside traditional limits:

> A narrow definition of library scholarship limits academic librarians' scholarly activity to explicitly library science topics. Examples include bibliometrics, information literacy pedagogy, and evidence-based management research. . . . An expanded definition of library scholarship includes scholarship and creative and professional activity outside of library and information science, for

the library serves the entire college or university. Here librarians may be publishing in non-LIS journals or other periodicals, producing culture rather than documenting it, collaborating with other departments in grant writing or teaching of non-LIS topics, and performing professional work. Part of expanding the definition of library scholarship and work is about meeting the needs of the institution rather than just the library system. Higher education is changing, and librarians have much to offer. It seems reasonable to expect librarians with additional advanced degrees to utilize them to advance knowledge in those fields as well as to improve their job performances as librarians. (Thomas and Leonard 2014)

Others have proposed from the beginning that librarians have many difficulties. For some library problems, research does not always provide the most practical solution. Michael Buckland indicates that in libraries, just as in any situation where research is conducted, the "perceived importance of the problem" is what matters most. He proposes "five grand challenges": Can library services be made more meaningful? Who knew what and when? How neutral can libraries be? Have we designed digital libraries backward? And how do library communities differ? (Buckland 2003).

IDENTIFYING A RESEARCH AGENDA

What are the benefits of academic librarians engaging in research and publishing? The research provides many examples of the negatives—no time to devote to the research process; not enough funding to support the process and expenses that come along with it; and no formal training in effective research skills. But the positives include earning promotion or tenure; building your own area of expertise; sharing best practices; learning new skills and knowledge; and, of course, contributing to the knowledge base of our profession. So how does one find ideas for research and publication? The most common ideas come from day-to-day practice and operations. When a new technology, system, procedure, or service is implemented, it becomes an opportunity to review best practices for what worked and what didn't, comparison with peers, and new guidance. In addition, new, innovative responses to challenges; identification of trends; and management and leadership topics rise to the top.

In a 2016 article "Five Challenges Confronting Library-Related Research and Researchers," Peter Hernon identifies the components of the research process: The introduction "sets the stage for the problem statement, which places the spotlight on what will be examined, the uniqueness of the coverage, and the intended value of the research. If the goal is a study intended solely for local use, uniqueness is unnecessary." Next, the literature review "identifies, highlights, integrates, and, most importantly, relates relevant research to the declared problem," and then "the theoretical framework connects the research and guides the data" (Hernon 2016). Hernon notes that appropriate research topics can come from a variety of sources, including the individual's own curiosity, organizations with compelling priorities, journals, and professional associations, just to name a few. He also shares that there are some challenges to our future research efforts:

- Addressing new problems and conceptualizing old ones in new ways,
- Connecting research to conceptual or theoretical frameworks and doing so properly
- Being receptive to the existence and relevance of new methodologies
- Making connections to global research
- Acting on study findings applicable to planning and decision making

These challenges are also the areas of opportunity for creating one's research agenda.

CONCLUSION

There is some good news to report: While we are not yet where we need to be, efforts to support and improve our commitment to conducting research can be found in several ways within our organizations: writing and research groups to encourage and support the production of scholarship, mentoring programs that pair seasoned authors with those who are new to the process, proper amounts of release time, and funding for activities devoted to research. Specific examples of this include the following:

- IMLS's Institute of Research Design for Librarianship (IRDL), which provides continuing education opportunities for academic librarians to enhance their research skills and output and to increase the scope and value of academic library research (IMLS 2013).
- Review of the current LIS programs indicates more are including a research methods course, and nearly all have some version of research methods offered as an elective.
- Some academic libraries are creating research agendas and providing enhanced support of any library employee's research projects that connect with or integrate prioritized research areas (see IUPUI's Library Research Agenda as an example.

Regardless of where you stand on the issue of status, the three components of academic librarianship remain professional practice, scholarly contribution, and service to the profession. This is where we must continue to develop our efforts.

Chapter Four

Anchored in Service

"Many individuals who pursue a career in academia labor under the assumption that service is something that is disconnected from, and less important than, teaching and scholarship. However, in reality, service can be complementary to the other two endeavors, and I would argue, is actually essential if one is to ever become a well-rounded scholar. Service not only affords us the opportunity to share our knowledge and expertise with our students and our colleagues; it also encourages us to leave the ivory tower and engage with our community in a meaningful way."—Heather L. Pfeifer

The third anchor of academic librarianship is service to the profession through contributions, which could include institutional committee work, community service, and service in professional associations. This chapter reviews contributions to service and includes a discussion of the professional associations of our discipline, as well as the expansion that comes with the increased hiring of PhDs in other disciplines. For example, ALA membership information notes that only 4.5 percent of members hold PhDs, and anecdotal evidence suggests that in some cases, those PhD holders prefer to join professional associations within their PhD discipline. This means that their service contributions go to their discipline and not the library profession. If this is true, does it affect our definition of *service to the profession*?

SERVICE

Early in the history of higher education, academic faculty typically had an active role in the governance of the university and in fact claimed that participation in university decision making was (and still is) considered a right of the faculty role. That reasoning, according to some, stems from the basics of organization theory, which relates employees' job satisfaction with their ability to participate in certain types of decision making and with work productivity (Floyd 1985). Taking a different approach, Leonard Cassuto writes in "University Service: The History of an Idea" that the combination of teaching, research, and service used to be more focused on service rather than on teaching and research. He says, "[W]e need to go back to the age of the college in the United States, before research universities were founded" (Cassuto 2016). Cassuto cites the work of Donald Light, who breaks the work of early-nineteenth-century American professors into a different triadic division: the disciplinary career, the institutional career, and the external career (Cassuto 2016).

Cassuto (2016) explains that in the early-nineteenth-century era of the American college, "professors' salaries were often insufficient to cover basic needs, so many of them maintained separate careers outside the institution—as clergymen, for example—to make ends meet." In addition, faculty members spent their time doing whatever the institution required and were "responsible for their students' intellectual development [and] their 'moral and spiritual development,' . . . like a professor, resident adviser, class dean, and pastor all rolled into one. . . . Service was inseparable from teaching in this scheme" (Cassuto 2016). He says that the "formation of professional societies followed the birth of the American research university. . . . The creation of these disciplinary societies shows how the pursuit and organization of knowledge joined the emergent academic professionalism in the United States to form a newly professionalized ideology of higher education" (Cassuto 2016). This led to what Cassuto calls the "prestige economy," and it was during this period when service emerged as an outcome of the publicly funded institution and where the founder of a land-grant institution Ezra Cornell made the statement that ideally, the university should be a place "where any person can find instruction in any study," which in turn led to the ideal of "higher education as a public service, in which the university reaches out into the community at large" (Cassuto 2016).

Cassuto (2016) notes that the teaching-research-service triad first appeared in the 1920s and is credited to Marion Leroy Burton, president of the University of Michigan, who is quoted as saying, "[T]eaching, research, and service were concrete examples of the things that a university should make its chief aim." As the research university grew, departments were added to the organizational structure. Those departments needed administrators, and those administrators came from the faculty. Eventually, service within the university in this capacity replaced service to the community.

There is another reason for faculty in the academy to consider service within the university. It offers an opportunity to be involved in the decision-making process. Floyd (1985) writes that the rationale for faculty participation in institutional decision making rests on reasons for employees' participation in any organization. Participation in institutional decision making is associated with increased employee satisfaction and performance in a wide variety of organizations. That satisfaction and the quality of work life are now also increasingly viewed as valued outcomes. However, Floyd (1985) indicates that faculty tend to "accord legitimacy to and fully cooperate in the implementation of only those policies that faculty have helped formulate because they believe faculty have a right to participate." For library faculty, John H. Moriarty wrote in 1970 that membership on academic committees could be viewed as a measure of acceptance by the faculty and the administration. In addition, it is an important association of faculty status because it is one more way that the librarian can come to know his community.

Just as library faculty struggle to find broad acknowledgment of their status, they have struggled to gain acceptance or invitation to the inner workings of the academy. Questions also remain about incentives and rewards for such participation, which typically includes committee work, special assignments, program or even curriculum development, sponsorship within academic centers, and invitations to be part of other university activities or projects. Instead, many academic librarians tend to focus on service to the profession through activity in professional associations, where participation can influence the academic librarian personally and professionally. Some are able to participate in both the inner workings of the academy and via professional associations. What does that participation look like?

When a new academic librarian assumes their first professional position, they have much to decipher in addition to on-the-job performance. As I show in the next chapter, many have and continue to call for national standards for status, renewal, promotion, and tenure for academic librarians that would make requirements clearer. Without them, each new academic librarian will navigate those expectations within the institution they join. The breakdown between expected job performance load, contribution to research and scholarship, and service to the profession can range from 60/20/20 to 90/5/5 and everything in between. While the new librarian spends the majority of their time learning the job, they may have already developed a research profile in graduate school or have an idea of how their research and scholarship will be developed. If the individual has a second master's or a PhD, then the scholarship produced for that specialization could be the primary area of focus, or the job could offer a new opportunity.

While the debate of national standards continues, we can find the definitive "qualifications" for consideration of library faculty within the American Library Association (ALA), who defines in "A Guideline for the Appointment, Promotion and Tenure of Academic Librarians," was last approved at the ALA annual conference in June 2010. Section 2 discusses the qualifications of the library faculty:

> All activities shall be judged by professional colleagues on and/or off the campus on the basis of their contribution to scholarship, the profession of librarianship, and library service. The basic criterion for promotion in academic rank is to perform professional level tasks that contribute to the educational and research mission of the institution. Evidence of this level of performance may be judged by colleagues on the library faculty, members of the academic community outside the library, and/or professional colleagues outside the academic institution. (ALA 2010)

The ALA guidelines (2010) also indicate that evidence for promotion may include the following:

1. Contributions to the educational mission of the institution: for example, teaching (not necessarily in a classroom); organization of workshops, institutes or similar meetings; public appearances in the interest of librarianship or information transfer. Assessment by students and professional colleagues may contribute to this evaluation.
2. Contributions to the advancement of the profession: for example, active participation in professional and learned societies as a member.
3. Activities related to inquiry and research: for example, scholarly publication, presentation of papers, reviews of books and other literature, grants, consulting, service as a member of a team of experts, or other means of disseminating professional expertise.

Within the university, that guidance from the ALA for academic librarians is laid out generally in terms of university service or community service, as promotion committees are interested in seeing how one has contributed to the university above and beyond the duties of the job.

In "Professional Development Opportunities for New Academic Librarians," Robert K. Flatley and Michael A. Weber (2004) note that

> in addition to the benefits of serving the university, committees are a great place to network and learn the culture of your institution. It also elevates the importance of the library. You can use your membership as an opportunity to be an ambassador of the library and promote its resources and services. One author has used his membership on the University's General Education Committee to promote the need for information literacy and research skills in the curriculum.

They suggest that starting with library committees is a good way to ease into participation at the university level, which also allows others to benefit from your expertise and service. In addition, Flatley and Weber note that librarians have a core set of skills that include organization, public service, outreach, technology, and information literacy that many community organizations would find valuable:

Some suggestions for service include:

- Manage a local organization's library or archives.
- Serve on your local public library board or as a volunteer.
- Serve as webmaster for a local organization or become a LISTSERV moderator.
- Provide technical assistance to a local organization.
- Present a community lecture on local history, genealogy or research skills.

Using one's expertise in these ways can be very fulfilling both personally and professionally. (Flatley and Weber 2004)

THE AMERICAN LIBRARY ASSOCIATION

The American Library Association was formed on October 6, 1876, during the Centennial Exposition in Philadelphia. Orvin Shiflett (1981) writes that it

> gave focus to the development of professional distinctions among academic librarians. True, college librarians were neither a large nor important membership of the ALA until well into the twentieth century, the influence of men like Justin Winsor, librarian of Harvard from 1877 to 1897 and president of the ALA from 1876 to 1885, and the missionary zeal of Melvin Dewey, who, in addressing the 1891 meeting of the Middle States Association of Colleges and Secondary Schools, compared the library to "the college well, open to the students whenever they are in the mood to use it," incorporated a philosophy of service into the professional awareness of academic librarians.

Throughout his book, Shiflett shows how everything stopped or started by approval from the association: Functions and scope of academic library work weren't elevated until they were recognized by the ALA; the evolution of committees was based on member input; and the ALA offered "official sanction." Today's academic librarians have very different views of our professional association. When reading Shiflett and other articles and texts on the early years of the ALA, it becomes clear that somewhere along the way, they began to lose the confidence of its members. What happened?

Shiflett (1981) notes that the

> relation of the ALA and the public library movement to academic librarians was such that academic librarians did not attempt to establish concern for their own special interests within the association. Rather, they accepted the emphasis of the ALA and shared the interest in public library development. But many perceived that library education, conditioned as it was by the needs of the public libraries, was inappropriate for the special interests of academic libraries.

In Shiflett's (1981) interpretation, what happened is that the ALA's "missionary spirit of public library development" did not do us any favors in our efforts to "establish a consistent form as a profession."

Today, many questions, concerns, and calls for transformation surround our professional association. Some stem from the seeming unwillingness of our "oldest and largest library association in the world" to establish more stringent standards for membership. Indeed, these questions go back as far as the 1930s. In *The Maturity of Librarianship as a Profession*, Dale Shaffer (1968) writes that the

> ultimate test of a profession's willingness to make sure that its members are well prepared is the standard it sets for membership in its own associations. To date, there are no professional requirements for membership in the American Library Association. Any interested individual who works in a library may be admitted as a member. There is no specific requirement that he possess a bachelor's or master's degree in librarianship. This means that on the basis of interest alone he may vote, hold office, join in discussions of professional problems, and represent other librarians who have met much higher standards. (77)

This would be as if the American Medical Association allowed pharmacists, nurses, and other hospital workers to join the association, where currently only properly trained physicians are admitted. The exclusion adds a layer of status and credibility to the association that many say is missing from the American Library Association. Is status, though, the only reason academic librarians join associations?

This then begs the following questions: "What purpose leads academic librarians to join associations?" "Conversely, why do they choose not to?" "If they do join, is the focus on library-specific opportunities or beyond?" In 1997, *Library Trends* produced an issue devoted to these questions and more. In "To Join or Not to Join: How Librarians Make Membership Decisions about Their Associations," Sue Kamm tries to answer these questions. She notes that for those lucky ones where employers pay dues and conference expenses, it is an easy choice to select associations that are most relevant to the job. Most academic librarians don't have that luxury, though, requiring careful consideration before making a decision. In addition, unlike other professions that require professionals to participate in continuing education, librarians have no such national standard or obligation. Kamm created a brief survey to validate her perceptions and received 116 responses. In response to the question "What factors influenced your decision to join a professional association?" Kamm (1997) notes that the "opportunity to network with colleagues (94 respondents), the opportunity to make a contribution to the profession (78), and the quality of meetings or conferences (73) drew a higher number of replies than did the cost of dues (59)." In response to the question

"Why do you not belong to professional associations?" the cost of dues was cited most, followed by employers not paying dues or allowing time to attend meetings (Kamm 1997).

Most of the articles in the 1997 *Library Trends* issue note a lack of research on library associations, and I find that this continues to be the case. Between 1997 and 2019, most of the information regarding professional associations for academic librarians deals not with service to the profession; rather, the focus is on professional-development opportunities, value add for the individual, and whether the individual should consider opportunities for service outside the profession of academic librarianship. Agnes Bradshaw (2013) offers a perspective contrasting offerings both within and outside the profession in her chapter in *Revolutionizing the Development of Library and Information Professionals: Planning for the Future*. She notes that "professional librarian organizations are available on the international, national, state and/or local level. In 'National Trade and Professional Associations in the United States' there are 72 professional associations categorized under the heading 'Libraries'" (Bradshaw 2013). In addition, there are state associations and some states with more than one chapter, so that number is a bit higher. With plenty of opportunities to serve the profession, I go back to the question asked earlier: Do library faculty join associations, especially when the professional associations concerned with library and information science provide crucial components of the infrastructure for research in the field? The US Department of Education (1988) asserts, "They provide the means for communication, publication, and dissemination of the results of research. They provide the forums within which research issues can be identified and prioritized. They potentially can serve as means for influencing political policies related to research agendas."

Today, in 2020, there are new questions, concerns, and calls for transformation within our professional association, especially in light of two recent highly publicized events that will define how we respond and decide to move forward in our diversity, equity, and inclusion efforts. The first happened in 2019, when April Hathcock, director of scholarly communications and information policy at New York University, lawyer, and ALA Council member, shared a personal experience she had at a midwinter council meeting. April, who is Black, writes about a traumatic experience she had during a council meeting when she was "verbally attacked" by a fellow council member, a White man. She also notes in the post, "It turns out this ALA Midwinter was a doozy for people of color; several of us had to file reports on incidents of racist aggressions" (Hathcock 2019). April's courage led to more public reports by people of color on social media and a public apology by the association that notes future endeavors to create a better association (see ALA 2019a).

The second incident happened not within the profession but to a nation that watched in horror the death of George Floyd, a Black man, at the hands of police officers on television, in social media, and in the weeks-long protests around the world that followed. This event and Floyd's final words, "I can't breathe," led to renewed calls for the end of systemic racism that continue to plague our country. Following this incident, our library organizations and associations, like many others, issued statements denouncing racism and shared new guidelines, calls for change, and proposals for accountability. The ALA's most recent public response takes responsibility for past racism, pledging a more equitable association that all will be watching closely. Another chapter looks further into these incidents through the lens of our origins, systems of power, labor, and exclusionary practices.

INTERNATIONAL, REGIONAL, AND STATE ORGANIZATIONS

In addition to our hallmark national association, there are other ways that academic librarians can anchor into service for our profession vis-à-vis state, regional, or international options. Mary Wise (2012) writes that after the American Library Association was born, several states established library associations, and by 1905, twenty-eight states had created library associations. Wise also notes that there is little in the literature that demonstrates the benefits of belonging to and participating in state and regional library associations. Conducting a review of the fifty state associations and four regional associations, Wise (2012) categorized the priorities into six general areas: "Leadership, Support of Library Services, Professional Development, Library Advocacy, Intellectual Freedom, and Membership Acquisition." She also notes that some of the benefits of participation in the smaller state and regional associations include greater opportunities for attendees to meet people in similar career paths; more opportunities for leadership in committees and contributions; typically less costs; and easier navigation and meeting with vendors (Wise 2012). Today, according to the ALA website, all fifty states have state library associations (or chapters), as well as the District of Columbia, Guam, the US Virgin Islands, and regional library associations in the Mountain Plains, New England, Pacific Northwest, and Southeastern regions. The ALA's fact sheet indicates that there are more than 55,000 members today.

Beyond the ALA, there is the International Federation of Library Associations and Institutions (IFLA), and their website indicates that it is the "leading international body representing the interests of library and information services and their users. It is the global voice of the library and information profession" (IFLA 2019a). As of 2019, the IFLA has 1,500 members, representing more than 150 countries around the world. They are an "independent, international, nongovernmental, not-for-profit organisation" that aims to

- Promote high standards of provision and delivery of library and information services
- Encourage widespread understanding of the value of good library & information services
- Represent the interests of our members throughout the world (IFLA 2019a)

The website also notes that members join to build international professional networks, contribute to library work in one's area of expertise at an international level, decide what makes a global national agenda, and help find solutions to global problems.

SERVICE IN PROFESSIONAL ASSOCIATIONS

One attribute that defines a profession is the creation of a body of knowledge and theory, which must be continuously tested, revised, and expanded and creates a need for its members to constantly pursue the creation of new knowledge; "[t]hus one value an association can bring to its profession is to encourage and support research that feeds the theoretical/knowledge base of the profession" (Fisher 1997). An association can also encourage and support professional development for its members. Robert Holley notes in his 2016 article "Library Culture and the MLIS: The Bonds That Unite Librarianship," that professional organizations "have an important role to play in defining and promoting librarianship's cultural values." Holley (2016) also notes that the "diversity of types of libraries can work against a common culture. The prime evidence of this conflict is the multiplicity of library professional organizations. If some librarians or libraries as corporate bodies feel that their needs are not being met by a broad organization, they may form a more specialized group with a narrower mission."

Another attribute of a profession is that they include organizations that provide an opportunity to present a unified voice for its members. Shaffer (1968) explains, "Three aims of all such organizations are (1) to guarantee professional competence of their membership, (2) to guarantee professional conduct of their members, and (3) to raise the status of their professions." Although today there are many professional associations and organizations that a librarian or library worker may belong to, the American Library Association is the oldest and largest library association in the world. From their website we know that the mission of the ALA is "to provide leadership for the development, promotion and improvement of library and information services and the profession of librarianship in order to enhance learning and ensure access to information for all" (ALA 2019b).

Some issues members have with this flagship organization include a lack of standards or requirements for membership. Their website states, "ALA membership is open to individuals, organizations and non-profits, and businesses interested in working together to change the world for the better through libraries and librarians" (ALA n.d.b.). There are no specific requirements that an individual possess a bachelor's or master's degree in librarianship, which means that anyone who is "interested in working together" and pays the cost of membership is able to vote, hold office, join discussions, and represent librarians of all types who have invested in the professional requirements.

By contrast, other professions like the American Medical Association (AMA) and the American Bar Association (ABA) currently admit only appropriately trained medical and legal professionals, respectively. According to the AMA website, membership is open to physicians, residents, and medical students (AMA n.d.). A bit similar to the ALA is the ABA: According to the its website, one may join as a US-licensed lawyer, a non-US-licensed lawyer, a law student (at an ABA-accredited law school), astudent (postsecondary-education-level student), a recent law school graduate who has not yet taken the bar exam, or a nonlawyer (including paralegals, law librarians, economists, and others interested in the ABA) (ABA n.d.). The difference with the ABA is that they are more specific about who can join than the ALA is.

So how many academic librarians are members of library associations? In 1972, Virgil Massman wrote *Faculty Status for Librarians*, which includes chapters on faculty or academic status, problems and responsibilities of faculty status, benefits, and analysis related to those topics based on survey data. The survey questionnaires were sent in 1970 and returned by 224 of 281 academic librarians (80 percent), which were used in the analysis. Massman (1972) notes that 44 percent of librarians were members of ALA, and 83 percent of faculty librarians belonged to a national subject association. On the ALA website, the latest statistics are from 2017: 62 percent of members self-identified as having an MLS, 26 percent have a master's degree other than the MLS, and 5 percent have a PhD. This membership information supports the argument that PhDs tend toward their disciplinary associations.

NONLIBRARY PROFESSIONAL ASSOCIATIONS

The introduction to this chapter references professional associations associated with our discipline, as well as the expansion that comes with hiring more PhDs in other subject disciplines and the statement that most PhD hires don't contribute to library professional associations. The evidence for those statements comes from several sources. First, the ALA membership information states that 5 percent of ALA members hold a PhD. Anecdotally, in my institution, 6 percent of library faculty (promotion and rank, nontenure) hold PhDs, and all belong to their subject specialty associations and contribute research and scholarship through their specialty publications; none belong to the ALA. (Two of nine acquired an MLS, one before and one after receiving their PhD.) What's behind their reasoning?

While no quantitative data supports the anecdotal face-to-face conversations with a dozen PhD holders working in academic libraries, their responses were basically the same. Most indicated that even though they happen to work in an academic library, they strongly identify with their PhD subject specialty and sought positions as subject librarians, where they would also have opportunities to teach concurrently.

In a 2010 article, José A. Montelongo, Lynne Gamble, Navjit Brar, and Anita C. Hernandez propose another reason: that the "status and roles of librarians can be enhanced through the production of scholarly research, particularly scholarship in a field other than librarianship." They provide evidence that "conducting research, publishing in the subject disciplines, and becoming professionally involved in the scholarly activities of their subject disciplines not only benefits a subject specialist's own library, but also enhances the status, roles, and personal job satisfaction of individual librarians, the prestige of the particular library, and librarianship as a whole" (Montelongo et al. 2010). In addition, Montelongo and colleagues (2010) note that pursuing a nonlibrary research agenda "frequently" leads to publishing articles and presenting at professional conferences; these librarians are sought after for their expertise and provided other opportunities to be of service outside the field of librarianship. The benefits of contributions outside traditional librarianship, the authors note, are enhanced prestige for the library, influence on nonlibrary research projects, the potential to be viewed as creators and disseminators of knowledge, and a transformation of traditional perceptions. While all of that may be true, what the authors don't acknowledge is that separating library research from its roots denies the profession of librarianship; its history; contributions by its members; and, more importantly, its own chance to transform perceptions.

CONCLUSION

We continue to see the same unsettled views, unanswered questions, and suggestions about the inadequacy of our educational roots, particularly as they relate to our professional association. There are, however, signs of major transformations to come. In January 2020, the American Library Association announced the appointment of Tracie D. Hall as its executive director, effective February 24, 2020. According to the press release,

Hall is no stranger to libraries, or to ALA. Over the years she has worked at the Seattle Public Library, the New Haven Free Library, Queens Public Library and Hartford Free Public Library. In 1998, she was among the first cohort of ALA's Spectrum Scholars, a grant program to diversify librarianship, and she served as the director of ALA's Office for Diversity in the early 2000s. Most recently, Hall directed the culture portfolio at the Chicago-based Joyce Foundation, developing new grant programs designed to catalyze and scale neighborhood-based arts venues, cultural programming and creative entrepreneurship. A civic leader in Chicago, Hall was appointed to serve on the City of Chicago's Cultural Advisory Council at the beginning of 2020. Hall has also served in multiple roles in academia, including as assistant dean of Dominican's Graduate School of Library and Information Science in River Forest, IL. (ALA 2020)

Hall also happens to be the "first female African American executive director in ALA's history" (ALA 2020). This is a move in the right direction for this association. In addition to new leadership, the association itself is acknowledging the need for transformation. The 2017–2018 ALA president Jim Neal created a committee in June 2018 to

> carry out a comprehensive review and study of ALA's governance, member participation and legal structures and systems, with the goal of proposing changes that will vitalize its success, strength and agility as a 21st century association.
>
> The Steering Committee on Organizational Effectiveness (SCOE) will provide advice and support to the Executive Board on priority improvements. The work of the Steering Committee will focus on membership development and engagement, and on encompassing the diversity of voices that enrich ALA through incorporating the perspectives, interests and contributions of a wide variety of stakeholders and affiliated groups. Its work will be mission driven and embrace the Association's core values. (ALA Forward Together n.d.a.)
>
> The charge is to develop and recommend strategies and tactics to create an ALA with the agility to respond to current challenges and opportunities, and to focus energy and resources on its mission and members in the decades to come. Ultimately, it is to design a *modern association for a modern profession*. (ALA Forward Together n.d.a.; italics in original)

The Forward Together website acknowledges that the "only way that a member-driven organization like ALA can successfully move forward is through a member-led process that relies on broad member input, develops recommendations to incorporate member ideas, and sets the stage for member action and change" (ALA Forward Together n.d.b.). The challenge now is for members to generate results and real, transformational change to occur.

As important as our national association is to the continuation of our profession, acknowledging that service is and should continue to be an anchor for academic librarianship is even more important. Whether that service happens within the academy; within a specific discipline; or within state, regional, national, or international associations, what matters is that we serve in order to make things better for all of us.

Chapter Five

Education

"The multidisciplinary nature of libraries makes them unique modern institutions. If we can change 'multidisciplinary' to 'interdisciplinary' we have a powerful tool to develop an integrative educational role for the library, the place to go to 'put it all together.' Librarians could teach the impossible, e.g., integrating the knowledge from disparate discipline into a coherent life structure."—James F. Wyatt

When we talk about the stability of academic librarianship as a profession, many within our profession seem to believe it all comes down to the education we receive. Granted, the educational rigor of library science was not self-evident in the beginning. However, that does not apply just to librarianship. Even the most solidified professions today, like medicine and law, followed the same trajectory. In comparison, librarianship is still very young, and we are going through the same growing pains. We can and should study the depths of these older professions, for eventually, they evolved into the most rigorous fields of study. It is the evolutionary process—the commitment to continuous improvement and response to environmental factors—that defines great transformations. When we look for it, the evidence shows that the educational rigor; requirements; and yes, evolution can be found within LIS education.

Academic librarianship began from a less-than-prominent place in higher education. Many of us are familiar with the story of Daniel Coit Gilman, a librarian at Yale who complained to President Theodore Dwight Woolsey in 1865 what the exposure to the cold and damp library location did to his health and was offered no hope for change. President Woolsey's response was that the place "does not possess that importance which a man of active mind would actually seek; and the college cannot, now or hereafter, while its circumstances remain as they are, give it greater prominence" (Shiflett 1981).

Looking closer at the education of librarianship, Shiflett notes that things didn't change much by the close of the nineteenth century and that to properly understand the history of American academic librarianship, we have to have an understanding of higher education in America. He notes that whether a college library "prospered or suffered" was based on its value to the college, which also included the position of the librarian in the academic community (Shiflett 1981).

Higher education also had a tumultuous start as Americans moved across the country following what they believed to be new opportunities—and then back again to their roots. Religious sects in competition with one another founded colleges to establish influence, and natural catastrophes, "principally in the form of fire, felled many colleges before they could securely establish themselves" (Shiflett 1981). (See Hofstadter 1963, Rudolph 1962, and Tewksbury [1932] 1965 for more on the beginnings of American colleges and universities.) Even as colleges began to see the value of the library, it wasn't until the end of the first quarter of the nineteenth century that any improvement was possible. Shiflett (1981) explains,

> Retail stores operated by publishers were the principal means of distribution, and publishers exchanged their products with one another to give their stores a more diverse stock. As the century progressed, publishing and bookselling increasingly became more specialized, separate activities, and direct purchase from publishers became the standard method of stocking, along with various import channels.

This made it hard for college libraries to build collections of their own and led to an emphasis on the collection of rare materials.

Over the course of the nineteenth century, many were dissatisfied with the limitations of the college experience. Thus the "university movement" began, which "resulted in the establishment of graduate education and professional schools, the development of specialization at the undergraduate level, and the emergence of an academic profession" (Shiflett 1981). Shiflett (1981) notes that in the "half-century from the end of the Civil War to the early decades of the twentieth century, America came of age." This transformation of education also affected the libraries as the numbers of faculty needed to teach grew; the production and dissemination of knowledge grew; and the acquisition of primary resources became essential for academic research. Shiflett (1981) also reports that a "dramatic change in the financial situation of American higher education enabled institutions to meet the demand" for library materials, and George Works (1927) notes that some universities "increased their combined book budgets from $63,000 to over $441,000."

With some basic understanding of higher education, we can take a closer look at the experience of some other professions. In *Education for Librarianship*, a compilation of papers presented at a University of Chicago Library

Conference in 1948, Bernard Berelson (1949) refers to Ralph W. Tyler's two main characteristics of a true profession: a recognized code of ethics and techniques based on principles rather than routine. Tyler points out the ethics in medicine, which

> dedicates the doctor to the saving of lives and the protection of the health of the patient above all material and personal considerations. In the case of the clergy, the accepted ethical code dedicates the clergyman to the service of God and his parishioners above all selfish considerations. The ethical code for the teaching profession dedicates the teacher above all to seek the enlightenment of his students and to a sincere, honest search for truth, whatever may be its implications. (quoted in Berelson 1949)

Regarding techniques, Tyler notes that a profession includes basic principles that

> must be viewed in an increasingly larger context. Thus, the science needed by the profession must be continually extended to more basic content rather than restricted only to the obvious applied science. For example, medicine has increasingly come to recognize the interrelationship of nutrition, physiology, anatomy, biochemistry, and other more fundamental sciences which give a much broader basis for understanding a particular medical condition of a given patient. (quoted in Berelson 1949)

Finally, Tyler notes eight common problems of professional education and developments in educating the professions:

1. The confusion of professional and nonprofessional tasks; analyzing the occupation to identify the professional as against the nonprofessional tasks
2. The selection of students to receive professional education; selecting students in terms of demonstrated characteristics and abilities.
3. The neglect or omission of content that illuminates the ethics of the profession and content that provides principles of operation; the requirement, as a prerequisite or concurrently with the professional education, of a well-rounded program of general education.
4. Distinguishing ethical values; the construction of courses within the professional education program that show the relation of the profession to the broad goals and activities of society.
5. Teaching the fundamental principles upon which professional tasks are based so that they are understood in a broad context; analyzing curriculum content in terms of its actual functioning as generalizations or concepts to guide intelligent behavior in the profession.
6. The inadequate connection between theory and practice; the increasing use of courses in other fields that have important implications for

the profession; and building a closer and more appropriate connection between theory and practice.
7. The failure in most programs of professional education to carry the learning of students to a high level of effective performance, depth of understanding, and self-directed further learning; the working out of definite plans for continued education.
8. Confusion about the nature of advanced professional education or graduate work; defining more clearly two functions of advanced education—one for educating the scholar of the profession and the other for educating a high-level practitioner. (quoted in Berelson 1949)

In conclusion, Tyler notes the field of librarianship has a

> unique opportunity to contribute to the improvement of professional education. Its major purpose is among the most important of any profession, that of public enlightenment. It works both with ideas and with people. It is not only a social science, but it also includes elements of the humanities and of the natural sciences. Hence, adequate education for the profession requires both breadth and depth. (quoted in Berelson 1949).

With that in mind, how did education for the academic library professional begin? In 1907, the American Library Association's (ALA's) Committee on Training wrote library tract 9, *Training for Librarianship*, which states,

> While the most necessary preparation for librarianship, as for other professions, is a good general education, and the most necessary natural qualification is common sense, there is a technical side in the work of every institution for the mastery of which neither a general education nor common sense is sufficient equipment.
>
> There are records to be kept, methods to be devised or learned, small, daily needs to be met by devices of one kind or another, books to be selected and bought and made useful; rules to be considered, ways of attracting and holding readers, ways of raising money, of securing help; buildings and equipment to study,—indeed, there are more subjects of study and consideration than could easily be enumerated.

In addition, the proliferation of libraries led to the need for the creation of uniform methods and the founding of library schools, "which in one, two, three or four years will prepare the satisfactory student to take his or her place in the library world, more or less well equipped to deal with the questions that arise in all libraries" (ALA Committee on Training 1907).

Along with a college education, the early ALA Committee on Training (1907) captures the pros and cons of summer library schools, apprentice classes, and correspondence courses:

Librarianship as a calling has several distinct advantages for the man or woman of good education, desiring to be of service, who is fond of books and who has executive ability. While it does not appeal to those who gauge all callings by their money returns, the librarian, if equal to his position, is associated with all the forces that make for social and educational improvement and is recognized as working for the community rather than for himself. For the individual who loves books it offers the privilege of working in the atmosphere of books, and of communicating his enthusiasm to others and putting his knowledge of books at their service. For the possessor of executive ability, work requiring personal initiative is always almost its own reward, and a library offers many opportunities for the exercise of such a gift. For one, who, in addition to these endowments, has the wish to help and serve others, there is no better field and few in which intelligent work is more needed.

STRUGGLES

In an effort to take a stand and define a new process for librarianship, the American Library Association redefined the early credentials to determine a "librarian." This process was coined the "MLS project" by Boyd Keith Swigger in his 2010 book *The MLS Project: An Assessment after 60 Years*. The intention behind redefining these credentials was to "embody a commitment by the ALA and library schools to recognize the MLS degree as the first professional credential and to limit ALA accreditation to master's degree programs" (Swigger 2010). That was step 1; step 2 was "taken formally in 1970 when the ALA adopted the policy statement 'Library Education and Manpower,' which distinguished professional work done by librarians—work that called for education in accredited master's degree programs—from nonprofessional work done by support staff" (Swigger 2010). Based on the level of questions that continue to arise sixty years later, it would appear as if these redefinitions did not quite do the trick, and Swigger's observations came to the same conclusion. He writes that data collected "from a variety of sources show that the MLS project has had limited success. Changing the level of the accredited degree did not produce the anticipated rewards for graduates of library schools" (Swigger 2010). Others also had opinions about the state of formal library education.

Patricia Paylore, an assistant librarian at the University of Arizona, in her presidential address at the 1956 Southwest Library Association conference, said she believes that "contemporary formal library education has taken the heart out of librarianship" (Paylore 1957). She expects a formally trained librarian to be "knowledgeable about books . . . willing to learn continuously . . . professional, in the highest and most dedicated sense, about his job, whatever it may be" (Paylore 1957). She shares experiences that indicate to her that library education at the time was shelling out a "breed of librarian which lack[s] spirit, gumption, faith," and she is concerned that librarianship was not producing people who learned the techniques, principles, or spirit (Paylore 1957). In her concluding remarks, she notes that she wants

> only that we bring more realism on the one hand and more spirit on the other, to the profession and that, in the doing, we rededicate ourselves, paradoxical though it may seem, to Milton's expression of the purpose of education: that it fit a man to perform his offices, both private and public, justly, skillfully, and magnanimously. If we are disenchanted with the products of our professional schools as they have evolved over the last generation, let us admit it, first of all, then seek to re-establish the firm bases for our own re-education. (Paylore 1957)

In *The Maturity of Librarianship as a Profession*, Dale Shaffer (1968) notes that the evolution of education for librarianship has four major periods. The first is pre-Dewey, which covers the time before Melvil Dewey established his School of Library Economy at Columbia College in 1887. In this period, public librarians and university and college librarians were trained based on their previous education level, and retired professors were assigned the responsibility for running the library. Shaffer (1968) explains, "Instructional content was defined by the tasks then performed in libraries, and methods followed actual or simulated field conditions." In the second period, defined as the time between Dewey and World War I, separate library schools were established. Period 3 dates from the publication of Dr. Charles C. Williamson's report of library trainings available in 1923 to a revised curriculum and degree proposed in 1948. The fourth period, from 1948 to 1968, is "characterized by experimental changes in the curriculum and degree structure of library schools" (Shaffer 1968).

In the fourth period, a recommendation for the core program for all librarians included classes on

- the library in society,
- professionalism,
- materials,
- services,
- administration,
- communication, and
- research.

For the most part, those topics did become core to the education outline of future programs.

Despite the many problems and recommendations cited in Charles Williamson's *Training for Library Services Report* (1923), the criticism of library education persists. Lawrence Clark Powell remarks in his paper presented at the 1948 Library Conference at the University of Chicago that for a "good many years the library schools have been the whipping boys of the profession. Williamson gave it to them good back in 1923, followed by Reece, Munn, Mitchell, Metcalf, Butler, Carnovsky and others—a series of indictments, confessions, reforms, and reorientations blessed by the angel of the Carnegie Corporation" (in Berelson 1948).

In his very thorough historical review of the education of academic librarians, Shiflett (1968) includes criticism of the formal library education plan, which left academic librarians "conspicuously absent from any special consideration in planning." He says that the

> failure of academic librarians to develop a formal preparation for their specialized area of librarianship derived in part from their failure to isolate a unique area of research. Rather than promote research into library operations or library problems, academic librarians generally agreed that systematic bibliography was their special province and concluded that bibliographic compilation should be the vehicle through which their scholarship would be recognized. But this level of research failed to win the academic community's support as evidence of sufficient scholarly attainment.

The "fundamental problem of librarians" in the struggle, according to William J. Goode (1961), is the "knowledge base on which the occupation is built." He says that there appear to be no clear standards around how much librarians should know and what they should know and admonishes that it is "difficult to define a problem for whose solution one would uniquely go to a librarian" (Goode 1961). In conclusion, Goode (1961) notes that the

> increasing flow of knowledge and the greater dependence of a technological society on our accumulation of knowledge will augment the economic bargaining power of librarians. This in turn will heighten the caliber of recruits as well as make it possible to require them to undergo more formal education in the decade to come. . . . More money will be spent on library research to develop the knowledge base of the occupation. Perhaps in time a new occupational category may be created—"research librarian"—someone who devotes his career to library research. Librarians themselves have urged these and related changes, which will in fact improve somewhat the position of the profession.

All three of these things have happened, and yet . . .

In "The 97-Year-Old Mystery Solved at Last: Why People Really Hate Library Schools," Samuel Rothstein (1985) notes that the criticism comes from everywhere—students, practitioners, surveyors, and library educators—and has been ongoing from the start. His article includes "An Anthology of Abuse: 97 Years of Criticism of Library Schools"—a thorough review of dozens of references. In the end, after presenting five theories based on his literature review, Rothstein offers another theory beyond resistance to change, inferior instructors, inevitable criticism, critics letting off steam, and "boring" education. His theory proposes that we think poorly of ourselves and that "library education and library practice do not create attitudes and values but are merely the arena in which they are displayed ready-made" (Rothstein 1985). What, then, are we to do? We can explore several options.

In 1990, we were still playing "what's wrong with our library schools," as Lawrence W. S. Auld calls it in his May 1990 *Library Journal* article. He also notes that we spent more time focusing on what's wrong rather than what's right. In the article, he notes seven imperatives: The first is the "opposing tensions between professional expectations on the one hand and academic expectations on the other" (Auld 1990). The second indicates that curriculum development and revision of the "new" information science components is needed. The third, Auld (1990) writes, is that resolution of the questions around undergraduate programs would be the "deliberate inclusion in all courses of consideration of how the different levels of library employees interact with each other and rely on each other." The fourth imperative admittedly provides no easy solutions but notes that minority recruitment should be a priority. Similarly, the fifth indicates that our curriculum design should "recognize a wider range of practices" to acknowledge the differences in librarianship around the globe (Auld 1990). The sixth and seventh address concerns about the size and organization of library schools and the differences between "general-purpose" and "single-purpose" programs. In other words, the small number of library schools at the time offered a range of courses covering all types of libraries and services with small numbers of faculty. Auld (1990) closes with his suggestions that before proposing significant changes, we should talk to library school faculty and students, request feedback from stakeholders outside the library who can provide suggestions, and include active participation by librarians in the accreditation process.

In a 2004 *Library Journal* article titled "Fixing the First Job," Ria Newhouse and April Spisak, new MLS grads, made a project out of their frustration with adjusting to their careers. The authors came up against "bureaucratic brick walls and resistance to new ideas for libraries" in the first year on the job (Newhouse and Spisak 2004). They created a survey and shared the reactions of 124 new librarians (defined as on the job for a year or less). Most (55.6 percent) agreed that library science classes prepared them well and taught them skills that they use on the job. Questions regarding graduate school programs and library practice revealed

> drastic differences in quality and tremendous variety among American Library Association (ALA)-accredited LIS programs. Programs require a range from nine months to 2.5 years of study. The most expensive program charges $43,000 a year, yet in-state tuition at publicly supported universities is frequently less than $5000 a year. Most programs have two to three required

"core" courses. A few had no required courses, while others required as many as six. (Newhouse and Spisak 2004)

In addition, a majority of respondents named specific classes they wish had been offered, including cataloging, budgeting, programming, readers' advisory, management, fundraising, grant writing, marketing, advanced reference, patron services, conflict management, and policy development. Almost every respondent indicated that they wished the program provided more practicality and less theory (Newhouse and Spisak 2004).

ACCREDITATION

Boyd Keith Swigger (2010) writes about the ALA accreditation process and its lengthy transformation:

> In 1992, after a three-year process of review and consultation by COA [Committee on Accreditation], and in accordance with the dominant trend among the regional accrediting agencies, the ALA Council adopted a new set of standards that focused on institutional goals, measures of effectiveness, and consultative processes. The 2008 revision of the Standards strengthened that emphasis.

ALA indicates the importance of the accreditation process to the future of the profession, noting its benefits as public assurance "that individuals who have graduated from accredited schools or programs have received a quality education," that accredited programs "meet the standards of the profession that they seek to enter," and that the institutions "benefit from self and peer evaluation and through the opportunity for continuous improvement" (ALA n.d.a.). The process report on the ALA website indicates that accreditation does not result in ranking of programs;

> Rather, it respects the uniqueness of each program while ensuring that all accredited programs meet the same standards.
> The accreditation process involves the continuous assessment and evaluation of a program and the enhancement of the program's operations using standards. This process, through self-evaluation and peer review, is designed to foster collegial relations among educators and members of the profession. Accreditation indicates that a program demonstrates a commitment to quality and that the program seeks to continue that commitment.
> The accreditation process and activities of the ALA's COA are founded on principles of accreditation (see Section I.3 for the principles). In the spirit of continuous improvement, the standards, procedures, and documents for ALA accreditation are periodically revised and updated as part of the effort to ensure optimal benefit to the profession and the public. (ALA 2012).

In addition, Ann E. Prentice (1992) writes in "Professional Programs in the University: A View from Not Quite the Top" that these policies, processes, and procedures are

> not just formalities to be endured, they are questions whose answers will determine that program's future.
>
> 1. How does the library and information science program contribute to the university's mission, and is it central to that mission?
> 2. Does it have an appropriate balance of teaching, research, and service?
> 3. Is it accountable for the quality of its programs, its students, and its other contributions to the university?
>
> If, after reviewing your accreditation report, program review, and state-mandated accountability measures, and relating this data to your plan and budget, the answer is yes (and this *yes* must come from outside the program as well as from inside), then your small professional school has a fighting chance to continue. Nothing is guaranteed, but you can stay at the university so long as you continue to justify your presence.
>
> If, however, the program is judged to be out-of-date and not dynamic, if its contribution to the university's mission does not justify continuation, if there will be little harm to other programs if it is discontinued, or if it is in danger of losing its accreditation, then it is fairly certain that the program will not survive. (Prentice 1992)

REVIEW OF ALA AND CERTIFICATION

Lori Bowen Ayre's article in *Collaborative Leadership* from 2015 outlines continuing education (CE) requirements for other professions, noting the following:

- Lawyers are required to get twenty-five CE hours every three years in California.
- Nurses in Michigan must complete twenty-five hours, with at least one hour in pain and symptom management, every two years.
- Pharmacists are required to complete fifteen hours per year in some states.
- Alabama architects must complete twelve CE hours on health, safety, and welfare topics per year.

Ayre (2015) writes that it is time to "re-professionalize the profession" and those requirements would, for one, help ensure that librarians navigate new technologies, performance measures, advocating appropriately, and fundraising, for starters. She also notes that the ALA website doesn't have much information about continuing education, except for "dead links, a reference to an old, unrealized action goal ('By 2005, ALA will be a leader in continuing education for librarians and library personnel'), and numerous mentions of conferences. Evidently, attending library conferences is our profession's idea of continuing education" (Ayre 2015). Five years later, the ALA "Continuing Education" page, under "Tools, Publications, and Resources," states that continuing learning is "critical to renewing the expertise and skills needed to assist patrons in this information age. Library workers must continually expand their knowledge in order to keep up with the rate of change" (ALA 2013b). The page indicates that there are "numerous continuing education opportunities" available, the importance of having CE offerings evaluated according to standards set by the International Association for Continuing Education and Training (IACET), and that ALA was awarded "authorized provider" status.

It was interesting to note that all the ALA pages regarding continuing education, certification, and standards have not been updated since September 23, 2013. Under "Certification and Licensure," the association acknowledges a "long history in accreditation" and that it has "historically not been involved with the certification of individuals." It also indicates that the question comes up "periodically" along with the definition that certification "attests to the possession by an individual of a specified body of knowledge and/or skills" (ALA 2013a).

CERTIFICATION

The calls for our professional association, or someone, to provide certification requirements continue. Dale Shaffer's 1968 discussion defined it as the "method used by the state to grant an individual the legal right to practice a specified occupation. Certification of librarians is the action taken by a legally authorized state body to recognize, on the basis of standards adopted by the body, the professional or technical qualifications of librarians serving in publicly supported libraries." It is a "license issued by the authority stating that the holder is qualified to hold a library position of a specified type or level" (Shaffer 1968). The objectives of a certification are assurance; protection; establishment of standards; aid in attaining professional status, prestige, and wage; encouragement to improve; encouragement to enter the field; and standards comparable to other major professions (Shaffer 1968).

Certification of librarians has been a matter of heated debate in our profession for nearly as long as our education programs have been around. Those who support it do so for a variety of reasons: a "desire for more uniform standards statewide; accountability issues relative to direct state aid to libraries; increasing or improving the view of librarianship as a profession; continuing education to keep the profession current; supplemental education in areas not addressed by preservice education; and an end-goal of improving service to the public" (Watkins 1998). Those who oppose certification do so because they feel it is "distracting and unnecessary" (Nussbaumer 2005). Neither side has been able to reach a consensus. In a 2012 paper, J. P. Bell indicates that "[s]upporters of certification appear insecure about the librarian's evolving role, fail to consider the expansive bureaucracy certification would create, and, in the end, offer no compelling evidence to require certification." And in response to those who equate ours with those of the law and medicine, Bell (2012) cites evidence that the

> frequent comparison to post-graduate credentialing for lawyers and doctors is dismissed on the grounds that those certification/licensing requirements act as insurance against liabilities inherent in those professions. One's ability to grasp volumes of updated case law and current medical literature and procedures, for example, will reflect directly upon the effectiveness of the legal or medical services provided (Estabrook, 1977, p. 218). In this way, certification and licensing of lawyers and doctors "contribut[e] directly or immediately to [protecting] life or welfare" (Jordan, 1948, p. 111). Drawing a keen distinction, Griffiths and King (1986) observed: "Unlike many other professions, however, the information profession can be said to provide *an intangible service* that rarely leads to a product or result obvious to the service recipient, let alone a standardized product" (p. 343, emphasis added). It would be dubious to claim that the provision of information is a matter of life and limb (though it might be on rare occasions). Opponents therefore dismiss calls for post-graduate certification and the presumption that it ensures high quality service based on the priorities of the law and medical professions as overwrought hyperbole.

REVIEW OF CURRENT MLS EDUCATION

Turning now to library school curriculums, programs, and transformation, there is mounting evidence that the message has been received. There are examples of change beginning in the mid-1990s through today. In January 1997, Deanna B. Marcum shared the results from grant funding by the Kellogg Foundation to transform library science curricula at the University of Michigan; Drexel University; the University of Illinois, Urbana-Champaign (UIUC); and Florida State University. The goal of the grant was "to test the notion that an infusion of funds would help schools of library and information science transform themselves into agents of change and overhaul their curricula with an eye toward the requirements of the future" (Marcum 1997). Evidence of change based on the grant at the University of Michigan included the recruitment of new faculty "to create specializations in information systems management, human-computer interactions, librarianship, archival and records management, and future systems architecture" (Marcum 1997). New courses and a new curriculum include foundation courses that are integrated and multidisciplinary and a "practical engagement requirement" to "ground academic studies in real-life settings" (Marcum 1997).

At Drexel, a new curriculum was devised to directly incorporate job requirements into courses; balance technical and human skills; and include new expectations for "cognate courses in psychology, computer science, mathematics, and composition" (Marcum 1997). UIUC's new course offerings "now carry titles that suggest the social, systems, organizational, and access issues of information work," along with a variety of technology options allowing students to earn the degree while being "almost entirely separated from a physical space" (Marcum 1997). The University of Illinois broadened the curriculum with the addition of more "problem-based learning" and a focus on fully reshaping the curriculum. Finally, Florida State University used the funds to create an undergraduate program that "focuses first on the user" (Marcum 1997).

In more recent years, we can find other examples of curriculum revisions. For example, more core curriculum requirements include some form of research methods, internships, fieldwork, or practicums. New areas of concentration include digital stewardship, data science, data and asset management, and critical librarianship. Course titles reveal acknowledgment and understanding of such new areas of focus as GIS, crisis informatics, project management, managing makerspaces, metadata management, and user experience. And at the University of Wisconsin, Madison, students have the option to "enhance their degree with a certificate in Innovation and Organizational Change or Leadership" (Grad School Hub 2020).

When it comes to ranking our graduate programs in library and information science, people commonly refer to the *US News and World Report* rankings; however, there are multiple ranking options available for consideration. In addition, there are websites like Masters in Library Science (https://www.mastersinlibraryscience.net) that propose readers reconsider choosing a program based on rankings. The website also looks at the most recently released rankings from *US News and World Report*, puts their own spin on the research, and notes that the rankings did not change when they accounted for location, accreditation, and whether they have an online MLS program. How are those rankings made, though?

US NEWS AND WORLD REPORT

The 2017 *US News and World Report* ranks fifty-one master's degree programs based on the responses to a survey sent in fall 2016 to each program's dean, director, and a senior faculty member. This ranking system is based on peer assessment questionnaires that ask individuals to rate the academic quality of programs at other institutions on a scale of 1 (marginal) to 5 (outstanding). Individuals who were unfamiliar with a particular school's programs were asked to select "don't know." Scores for each school were totaled and divided by the number of respondents who rated that school. The University of Illinois (UIUC) ranked number 1; University of Washington, number 2; University of North Carolina (UNC), Chapel Hill, number 3; Syracuse University, number 4; and the University of Texas (UT), Austin, number 5.

GRAD SCHOOL HUB

Grad School Hub (2020) compiles the twenty-five best master's degrees in library science for the 2019–2020 academic school year based on public data released from educational, commercial, and government databases. Their rankings are based on information gathered from five weighted categories: 20 percent from alumni feedback, 20 percent on continued enrollment, 10 percent on degree selectivity, 25 percent graduate expenses, and 25 percent on projected annual salary. Their rankings put the University of California, Los Angeles (UCLA), at number 1; UNC, Chapel Hill, number 2; UIUC, number 3; UT, Austin, number 4; and the University of Wisconsin, Madison, number 5.

COLLEGE CHOICE

According to their website, College Choice "helps students and their families find the college program that meets their particular needs" (College Choice n.d.). They maintain an understanding that each student is different and have developed tools like "Degree Finder, which generates a personalized list based on your preferred degree level and subject. College Choice offers resources to help students make informed decisions at every step along the way. We also offer admissions advice, scholarship information, financial aid information, and research guides" (College Choice n.d.). In order to determine the best library science programs, they start first with the academic reputation of each degree program and then look at student retention rates, affordability, and early salaries of graduates. To determine their final rankings, they note that information comes from program websites, PayScale, the nationally recognized *US News and World Report*, and the National Center for Education Statistics. Finally, their methodology includes affordability (30 percent), return on investment (ROI) (40 percent), and commitment to graduate education (30 percent) as the three primary categories for consideration of graduate programs. This website ranks UIUC number 1, Rutgers University number 2, Drexel University number 3, Catholic University of America number 4, and the University of Washington number 5.

Between the three ranking systems, UIUC is number 1 with *US News and World Report* and College Choice, while Grad School Hub gives UCLA the top spot. UIUC's website says that it takes forty credit hours to achieve the master of science in library and information science, will cost $15,000 in state or $28,000 out of state, and can be completed either residentially or online. There are two required courses: "Information, Organization, and Access" and "Libraries, Information, and Society," and while a research course isn't required, it is offered. In addition to the more traditional courses, they offer such courses as "Social Justice in the Information Professions," "Naming and Power," "Data Mining," and "Linked Data Processing."

In a conversation with a recent UIUC grad about what makes it a top-ranking program, they shared that for them, the "self-integration of the libraries and the library school mean that you not only are working with excellent faculty, but that there are many practical learning opportunities within the libraries for students at all levels, providing students with opportunities to learn all aspects of librarianship." They provided several specific examples of this, including a "Collection Development" course, where they "were able to actually take part in a real-time weeding (which we live-tweeted so those who couldn't be on campus in our hybrid meeting could participate)," and a preservation course, where they "were able to spend time working with materials and seeing lab technicians and conservators handle materials." In closing, they note,

> Not only did we have world-class faculty (both on campus and in the hybrid program), we also had lots of opportunities to use the libraries themselves and learn from the faculty and staff who are professionals as they worked. The scale on which this happens is so much deeper and broader than any of the other programs I looked at, precisely because of the size of the program. Its venerable status (I think the LEEP program, now their hybrid to completely online program, was the first of its kind in the country) also means that they have built a lot of infrastructure in the library school that allows them to make use of any adjacent disciplinary faculty throughout the university.

The University of Michigan's School of Information rounds out the top ten, and according to Degree Query, the School of Information is known for its

> multidisciplinary educational approach that combines a focus on both the human users of information and the technology of managing information resources. Due to its focus on incorporating practical experience and research into classroom studies of theory and principles, the University of Michigan's School of Information is considered "the first iSchool in the world to offer an integrated Master of Science in Information degree." (Degree Query n.d.)

The American Library Association website lists ninety accredited SLIS programs; thirty-seven have been discontinued (six restarted later and have a current program); and a fairly steady rate of candidacy requests for accreditation (currently Old Dominion University and University College London are listed with an accreditation decision in January 2022 and June 2023, respectively). A review of all programs indicates that one-third include some form of research methods course as a requirement; all but three of the current programs offer a research methods or design course, and a half-dozen "strongly recommend" the research course for those in the academic librarianship track. This alone seems to address the criticism from Hernon and others in the 1990s regarding the lack of research emphasis in our education.

Evidence of the changes to programs can be found in personal experiences by recent graduates. In a 2016 article, Alison Peters writes,

> My MILS education gave me the education and tools I need to learn how to thrive in the library and information world, and it also introduced me to phenomenal librarians who imparted their knowledge to me and gave me invaluable experiences I will take with me for the rest of my life. Like my internship with Canadian nonprofit Librarians Without Borders, who partner with libraries and librarians in developing areas to provide training, resources and support so under-served communities can have books and libraries of their own.

A 2020 Indiana University Purdue University (IUPUI) library school graduate shared her excitement postgraduation. When asked why she decided to pursue a master's in library science, she wrote,

> I pursued my MLS degree for a number of reasons, but chief among them was the idea that it opened the most doors for me. It has helped me incredibly in my current staff position in higher education, and I'm certain it will help me should I ever leave for another job or career. I also pursued my MLS because of my twin interests in rare materials and digital materials and digital preservation efforts; only in the MLS program could I find a way to combine those into a fruitful and educational experience. I've recommended the MLS field, and my specific MLS program, to a number of people because of the value that I see in it. A Masters in Library Science teaches students to look at the library—the physical embodiment of the pursuit of knowledge—from a number of perspectives, including materials and personnel management, research, development, and patron engagement. It also gives inquisitive minds the opportunity to explore issues that should be known to everyone, such as literacy efforts, societal engagement, diversity, and First Amendment issues, such as censorship and the Freedom to Read.

More reports share how library school programs are reviewing their MLS programs. In 2014, the University of Maryland's i-School reviewed their MLS programs. In the "Executive Summary," they note the reasons for the timing: societal changes, including the economy and a workforce with the need to shift their skills; major technological advances; ubiquitous information; and communities with shifting demographics. The initiative was launched to answer the following questions:

- What is the value of an MLS degree?
- What does the future MLS degree look like?
- What should the future MLS degree look like?
- What are the competencies, attitudes, and abilities that future library and information professionals need?

Their findings suggest that library professionals "need to be collaborative, problem solvers, creative, socially innovative, flexible and adaptable, and have a strong desire to work with the public." The MLS curriculum needs to "balance aptitude with attitude," and the next generation of information professionals "must thrive on change, embrace public service, and seek challenges that require creative solutions." Finally, the future of our profession "belongs to those who are able to apply critical thinking skills and creativity to better understanding the communities they serve today and will serve 5–10 years down the road—and those who are bold, fearless, willing to take risks, go 'big,' and go against convention" (Bertot, Sarin, and Percell 2015).

Their report also proposes areas for future curriculum design changes, including data management; digital asset management; assessment; policy; cultural competence; making (e.g., creation of makerspaces); and change. In a 2020 review of the current accredited SLIS programs, all the topics suggested by the University of Maryland's report could be found in other program course offerings.

CONCLUSION

It appears as if there will always be two sides to this story—we won't be able to convert everyone to the "MLS should always be required" debate. That isn't what this is about. What we should be able to agree on is that evidence shows our education programs are transforming and things are moving in the right direction, and things will continue to evolve. There is more work to be done, but we have some great examples of how to get it right—especially now, following a year when several global events have disrupted everything we thought we knew before. The University of Maryland report includes one final note, a "call to action" for the larger MLS community, where they propose a national summit on library and information science education. Together, let's accept that call to action and continue the good work taking place within our library and information science educational programs.

Chapter Six

A Path Forward

"Every craft, every trade, every art, every business, every profession introduces its literature and its knowledge. These literatures the library collects, stores, and lends to interested readers. Time was when the library considered its chief function to be storage. The time is now when the major function of the library is thought to be lending books. In the future, there is little doubt that the library will broaden the conception of its purpose and become the center of an educational enterprise which will seek to awaken, to attract, to invite, and to persuade the great mass of citizens into a better understanding of themselves and the world in which they live."—W. H. Cowley

At the end of his seminal work *The Maturity of Librarianship as a Profession*, Dale Shaffer (1968) provides a summary with eighteen main reasons librarianship was not and could not be a "highly recognized profession." Shaffer (1968) includes no uniform certification policy, the need for more systematic research within the profession, and that membership in the American Library Association remains open to anyone interested in librarianship. We have made progress fixing or eliminating nearly half of those over the fifty years since his book's publication. Those include a change in degree requirements: Today an MLS from an ALA-accredited library school is required. A specialized body of theory is provided through the formal classroom process, professional duties of the academic librarian are more clearly defined through job classification and description, and an effort to become highly professional minded has progressed (Shaffer 1968).

After the brief historical review in the previous chapters, it becomes clear that we are still a budding profession in many ways, still trying to work things out. Every profession collides with a challenge that propels the need to make disciplinary changes in pedagogy, certification, education, standards, general practice, and thought. Ours is no different. In 2020, we can't talk about the future of the academic librarian without also talking about the impact that systems of power and oppression; diversity, equity, and inclusion; critical librarianship (critlib); social justice; and open access are having on our future. In addition, all thoughts and discussions around transformation were cut to the quick with a devastating pandemic that hit the world just as 2020 was getting underway. And in the middle of that pandemic, the killing of George Floyd captured on video brought into the light something that people of color have known and experienced firsthand for too long—racial inequality.

At the beginning of the writing of this book, I created a framework to guide the subsequent chapters, including criteria, definitions, emergence of the profession, and formal educational requirements; professional and non-professional aspects and functions of academic librarianship; standards of status and certification; and suggestions for anchoring the profession into the future. Along the way, some early assumptions were confirmed, challenged, and demolished. Hopefully, we all know more now than ever before about the specifics of our future challenges and have some thoughts on how to address them.

Just knowing isn't enough, though, and 2020 shed a bright light on many things we've been ignoring at our own peril. Knowing and doing are two completely different things. It is time to take action. If we are serious about a metamorphosis into a fully robust, healthy discipline that addresses issues long left unresolved, then we must start making changes. The time is now. What follows is a list of trends that we ignore at our own peril, many of which have been shared in recent trends reports and forecasting exercises. In addition, there are issues that must be acknowledged, considered, discussed, and resolved once and for all in order for us to anchor into a path forward. And finally, there are proposals for consideration.

TRENDS AND FORECASTING

Artificial Intelligence (AI)

The academic libraries' response to automation and digital technologies has been debated for decades, and current events demand swift and decisive action. Historically, we tend to wait for new technology to become entrenched in the market before reacting and exploring ways it can work to our advantage. AI, often coupled with discussions of machine learning (ML), has dominated technology trends for years, but libraries have been slow to investigate or adopt their benefits. In 2019, Amanda Wheatley and Sandy Hervieux conducted an environmental scan of academic libraries' engagement with AI, and their findings indicate a lack of response or awareness to the current AI trend, though a small number of institutions were participating in or creating their own AI hubs (Wheatley and Hervieux 2019). Referencing a 2017 study by an Oxford University group looking at the future of the workforce in an AI-dominated world that indicates that librarians rank just above the median for "highly-computerizable" professions, Wheatley and Hervieux (2019) note that the "profession reacted as it did to most technological revolutions—it waited. In fact, it is still waiting."

In their literature review, Wheatley and Hervieux (2019) find research connecting AI to librarianship "quite low," despite the fact that it has been "expanding exponentially" in other fields:

> The absence of scholarly research on AI-related technologies in libraries is not to be unexpected. Libraries have suffered from issues on the adoption of digital technologies and a general resistance to change throughout the twentieth and twenty-first centuries. Library computerization had a slow upstart in the 1960s as automated internal processes started to emerge, but didn't fully take hold until the 1970s and 1980s. In comparison, the National Information Standards Organization was founded in 1939 and was already engaging in automation standards by the 1960s. The progression of industrial and office automation paved the way for libraries to adopt similar technology, yet this adoption was always years behind the current trends.

They note that such associations and organizations as the International Federation of Library Associations and Institutions (IFLA) and the American Library Association (ALA) are beginning to acknowledge the role AI will play in the future of librarianship. They also find that while no university or university library mentions artificial intelligence in their strategic plans, all universities in the sample offer courses on AI, and 81.5 percent sampled have research hubs focusing on AI. In contrast, only five university libraries of the twenty-seven in the sample offer programming and services related to AI. Very little collaboration between the libraries and other units within their institutions present missed opportunities for libraries to pave the way (Wheatley and Hervieux 2019).

The IFLA (2019b) notes that advances in artificial intelligence

> will enable a) next generation of web browsers to move beyond keyword analysis and evaluate the specific content of websites/pages (the semantic web); b) networked devices to combine speech recognition, machine translation and speech synthesis to support real time multilingual voice translation; and c) cloud based crowdsourced translation checking of webpage text.

This research could "revolutionize" search efficiency for users, with a positive impact on access to information and research productivity. They also acknowledge the negative implications of tracking, censorship, and content blocking.

And therein lies the problem: Traditionally, the technology that supports and enables our ability to access the mountains of information captured and "freely" available isn't really free. And in order to use it wisely, tracking, censoring, and blocking content are necessary evils that go against what librarianship stands for—privacy, opposition to censorship of any kind, and academic freedom. Yet it is for those very reasons that we must become leaders in the AI discussions within our academic libraries, our campuses, and our profession. There is some progress in this area within our library school programs. A 2019 review of course offerings about artificial intelligence found that Drexel; North Carolina Central University; San Jose State School of Information; Simmons University; University of California, Irvine i-School; and University of Southern California added course electives to their programs.

Big Deals and Open Access

This trend could also be called the "end of big deals." What is a "big deal" in academic libraries anyway? Kenneth Frazier, who coined the term *big deal* in a 2001 opinion piece, defines it as a "comprehensive licensing agreement in which a library or library consortium agrees to buy electronic access to all or a large portion of a publisher's journals for a cost based on expenditures for journals already subscribed to by the institution(s) plus an access fee." It's unsustainable. By 2018, an increasing number of universities were ending or threatening to end these bundled journal subscriptions with major publishers. Some institutions began to pay only for the journals they determined most necessary rather than subscribing to a bundled package that would often include duplicated journals or some that would go unused.

Why was the "big deal" so enticing to academic libraries? In a 2017 article, Rick Anderson writes that we embraced the deal for a couple of reasons:

> first, because the value proposition was so compelling in the short term, and the short term does matter; second, because it was clear even then that the scholarly communication ecosystem was in the middle of some kind of fundamental revolution, and there was no telling what it would look like ten or fifteen or twenty years into the future. In light of the massive short-term gain that the Big Deal offered us, we made a calculated bet that things in the publishing world would change sufficiently in the coming years to minimize the long-term risk.

Anderson says that warning voices were part of the problem because they were essentially "crying wolf" with their promises to cancel their big deals. In reality, most backed down when faculty members got wind of the impending cancellations, or they used it as a negotiation tactic, or they canceled but then accepted a new bundle deal when the content was noted as essential or the publisher offered a deal that was hard to resist (Anderson 2017). Anderson (2017) shares the results of his investigation of the status of big deals for thirty-one North American libraries: Twenty-four libraries canceled previous big deals, four canceled but resubscribed a few years later, and three announced they would be canceling but did not follow through.

The Scholarly Publishing and Academic Resources Coalition (SPARC) is a "global coalition committed to making Open the default for research and education. SPARC empowers people to solve big problems and make new discoveries through the adoption of policies and practices that advance Open Access, Open Data, and Open Education" (SPARC n.d.). It is no surprise, then, that they are tracking big deal cancellations, and they note six cancellations by some big-name research institutions, including Massachusetts Institute of Technology (MIT); State University of New York System (SUNY); University of North Carolina, Chapel Hill; and Florida State University. In 2019, the entire University of California System (UC) followed through on its threat to cancel their journal subscription deal with Elsevier. Their press release notes their reason for the cancellation: "Elsevier was unwilling to meet UC's key goal: securing universal open access to UC research while containing the rapidly escalating costs associated with for-profit journals" (UCLA 2019).

The trend is continuing, with more and more academic libraries canceling their big deals, and a new software tool, Unsub, is making that decision easier. What is Unsub and how does it work? The ACRL/SPARC Forum at the January 2020 ALA midwinter meeting hosted three panelists who "discussed efforts to negotiate with vendors regarding their 'Big Deal'" journal packages, including strategies and information that make such negotiations more effective for libraries" (Etschmaier, Sinn, and Priem 2020). Jason Priem, one panelist, described his company's product, Unsub, as a "data dashboard that helps libraries forecast, explore, and optimize their alternatives to the Big Deal, so they can unsubscribe with confidence" (Etschmaier, Sinn, and Priem 2020).

More information about Unsub can be found in an article by Dalmeet Singh Chawla (2020):

> Unsub, previously called Unpaywall Journals, was launched in November 2019 by Jason Priem and Heather Piwowar, co-founders of the scholarly services firm Impactstory. Funded in part by the U.K. charity Arcadia Fund, the project grew out of another tool the pair developed, called Unpaywall. Launched in 2017, it scours the web for versions of paywalled papers that are freely available on online repositories, preprint servers, and institutional databases, helping scholars circumvent paywalls legally. A 2017 study by Priem and Piwowar found that about half of the papers Unpaywall users sought were free to read somewhere on the web. But many librarians said they still weren't

clear on whether that finding meant they could scale back their subscriptions, Priem says.

Priem indicates that three hundred libraries already signed up for the tool, and he expected more cancellations in 2020 due to "cash-strapped universities" trying to weather the COVID-19 pandemic (in Chawla 2020).

Even with software tools like Unsub, big-deal cancellations have other consequences on open access. A case study by Anne C. Osterman, Sophie Rondeau, Jessica Bowdoin, Genya M. O'Gara, and James Pape (2020) notes that cancellations "affect the primary institution most, but they do not happen in a vacuum; it is important to consider them within the context of the academic ecosystem, particularly within preferred lending groups like statewide consortia." Their case study focuses on Virginia's academic library consortium and started "with the goal of better understanding the potential interlibrary loan impact on smaller institutions with limited funding that rely on their research institution partners for access to scholarly research" (Osterman et al. 2020). A key finding from their study is that the

> rate of requests filled from lending partners outside of Virginia for current years of cancelled publications is significantly larger than the requests filled from within the state, at least for a particular publisher with known low levels of statewide holdings. As more groups within Virginia and across the country cancel Big Deals, interlibrary loan turnaround time and costs have the potential to grow. In this context, the value of strategic sharing of titles with regard to both acquisitions and resource sharing cannot be overemphasized, and clarity in holdings and terms for loaning electronic content, with as much automation as possible, will be critical to efficient lending. (Osterman et al 2020)

They suggest that a "cooperative approach to journal acquisitions will be an important factor in minimizing the likelihood of a negative impact on researchers, as will improving discovery of Open Access content. A shared fund for document delivery services might also be necessary to help smaller institution researchers as easy access to no-cost interlibrary loan content diminishes" (Osterman et al. 2020).

Cox (2020) explains,

> Librarians have been lobbying for years to develop alternative pathways for research dissemination through institutional repositories and support of open-access publishing. This is the moment to advocate for open research and open data in federal grants and to educate faculty members about how to retain their publication rights. Look for libraries to also seek greater control of the research being produced at their institutions, as can be seen in the recent rise of publisher open-access agreements.

Indeed, a little over a year from the time that UC announced their big-deal cancellation with Elsevier, they "signed the biggest open-access (OA) deal in North America with one of the largest commercial scientific publishers. The agreement with Springer Nature includes a commitment by the publisher to explore making all articles that UC corresponding authors publish in the Nature family of journals immediately free to read on publication starting in 2022" (Brainard 2020). Look for more of these alternative pathways to open access in the future.

Critical Librarianship

According to Critlib, the "central homepage for an informal movement of librarians dedicated to exploring the issues of critical librarianship and social justice issues. Critlib is short for 'critical librarianship,' a movement of library workers dedicated to bringing social justice principles into our work in libraries" (Critlib n.d.). They aim to engage in discussion about critical perspectives on library practice. Their first post was published in 2006, and today they has an active Twitter feed, with conversations archived back to 2015. Kenny Garcia (n.d.) offers another definition in his ACRL "Keeping Up with . . . Critical Librarianship" blog post: Critlib "places librarianship within a critical theorist framework that is epistemological, self-reflective, and activist in nature. According to Elaine Harger, librarians that practice critical librarianship strive to communicate the ways in which libraries and librarians consciously and unconsciously support systems of oppression."

Garcia (n.d.) notes that critical librarianship is practiced in academic librarianship by applying a "critical lens" to our various assignments. He says that beyond critical information literacy,

> academic librarians and library staff are challenging regressive conceptions of gender identity in cataloging, excavating queer of color AIDS activist and trans archives, researching the misrepresentations of women, girls, people and culture in commercial search engines, documenting microaggressions in librarianship, and developing a diversity standards toolkit for academic libraries and librarians. (Garcia n.d.)

That challenge includes calling out and confronting microaggressions, confronting the implicit impact of power and privilege, and supporting underrepresented librarians and library staff and their diverse student bodies. However, some have criticized the movement. In "Interrogating the Collective: #Critlib and the Problem of Community," Nora Almeida (2018) writes that two of the most

> salient criticisms of #critlib are that the movement is exclusionary and, despite its counter-hegemonic and transgressive underpinnings, in danger of becoming

institutionalized. On the surface, these charges—that #critlib is on the one hand pervasive and on the other exclusive—are paradoxical. However, both rely on the assumption that #critlib constitutes a community and that the cultural values and ideas that #critlib has come to represent are grounded in that community.

Despite the criticisms, what we call the practice—the calling out, confrontation, support of these efforts, and resultant changes—are imperative.

ISSUES

COVID-19

In early March 2020, a pandemic shook the very foundation of everything that humans thought we knew and were prepared for. Along with the rest of the world, academic libraries were blindsided by the implications of a virus that acted swiftly with long-term consequences. When a nationwide lockdown was ordered to slow the spread, we quickly closed our facilities, moved services online, and transitioned our workforces to remote work. Everyone from shelvers to administrators worked hard to add value to the organization, safely, from home. We were able to shine in those areas where we've been working hard for years to curate, shape, and share digital content, and we developed and hosted strong web presences and intuitive search interfaces that could almost—almost—replace the human connection.

The impact for all of us will be felt for years to come as many questions were and continue to be raised, including library as place. Academic libraries suddenly shuttered their physical spaces due to growing concerns of the virus spreading through person-to-person contact, via air particles, and on surfaces of physical materials. As those spaces have begun reopening, it's time to consider the end. In other words, eventually, we will want all these people to return to the buildings, or "library as place," where we recently spent millions renovating to draw them back in. Or will we? If the answer is yes, then we need to think carefully about our responses to the current situation before demanding that users "keep out."

In addition to library as place, Christopher Cox (2020) writes that COVID has forced academic libraries to "face a paradigm shift." He predicts that the new landscape will highlight the diminishing value of print collections, the rise of "e-everything," increased digitization efforts of specialized collections, and copyright and fair use challenges. In addition, Cox (2020) predicts that "patrons won't visit us as much as they used to. We'll need to bring our services to them." Finally, Cox (2020) notes that employee safety, doing more with less, equity of access, and a whole new level of librarian activism will result from our time in quarantine.

The ALA and the ACRL worked quickly to provide statements on library closures and a commitment to supporting its members, staff, librarians, and library workers as the harsh realities of the shutdown included furloughs, the loss of benefits, or the loss of jobs as libraries closed. Academic library colleagues quickly created a way to gather information we could all use. By week 2 of the shutdown, Lisa Janicke Hinchliffe and Christine Wolff-Eisenberg "rapidly deployed a survey gathering real-time data from—and for—the academic library community. The survey, Academic Library Response to COVID-19, offered a snapshot of the solutions that libraries were putting into place on the fly, as well as existing processes repurposed to serve an unanticipated population of remote learners" (in Peet 2020). Hinchliffe and Wolff-Eisenberg (2020) shared their findings in several reports via Ithaka S+R blog posts; their final post from October 8, 2020, confirms some of the predictions made by Christopher Cox that employee care and safety, access to collections, and changes in services will continue to be part of our new normal.

Race and Power Systems

A review of the literature, including blog posts, Twitter feeds, and other social media ephemera, shows that we have been talking about diversity, equity, and inclusion (DEI) as it relates to practices, recruitment, retention, and community for a very long time (see the works cited in Hathcock 2015 for examples). And yet the needle has not moved much at all. This is definitely one area of our profession that *must* undergo a paradigm shift. When asked what the root cause of this slow progress is, many cite bureaucracy, lack of sufficient pipeline, or hard-to-move systemic practices. While those excuses may have pacified, we are no longer in a position where we can hide behind them.

For example, Dale Shaffer (1968) suggests increasing the professional status of librarianship "to increase the number of men in the field." He says,

> There are a number of reasons why a preponderance of females in librarianship tends to weaken it. First of all, the fact that the United States is regarded, at least sociologically, as a male dominated culture means that prestige is ascribed to those professions where males predominate. . . . Secondly, a stereotype of the old maid librarian has become fixed in the minds of many Americans. Lastly, voting in professional librarian organizations is to a great extent controlled by the female. This control means that new or controversial ideas tend to be voted down. For example, female librarians who are able to support themselves on $4,000 a year are reluctant to antagonize trustees about salary increases. Effort to achieve at least a balanced ratio of males to females in librarianship represents effort to raise the professional status of librarianship. (Shaffer 1968)

This example is not to say that Dale Shaffer had these solitary opinions; they were—and to a great extent still are—the cultural norms. We may have come a long way, but the predominant opinion remains that "prestige is ascribed to those professions where males predominate." Paula England, Andrew Levine, and Emma Mishel (2020) note,

> Social scientists have documented dramatic change in gender inequality in the last half century, sometimes called a "gender revolution." We show dramatic progress in movement toward gender equality between 1970 and 2018, but also that in recent decades, change has slowed or stalled. The slowdown on some indicators and stall on others suggests that further progress requires substantial institutional and cultural change. Progress may require increases in men's participation in household and care work, governmental provision of child care, and adoption by employers of policies that reduce gender discrimination and help both men and women combine jobs with family care responsibilities.

Note also that Shaffer makes no mention of including underrepresented groups anywhere in the monograph. In other words, power still lies firmly in the hands of White males, which is a systemic issue we must resolve.

How do we do that within academic librarianship? Christina Bell and Marisa Mendez-Brady (2017) write that we

> can and should challenge problematic professional norms such as the disciplinary impact of heteronormative and racist cataloging structures, the role of white supremacy in peer review processes, the discursive nature of citation styles, and a host of other scholarly mechanisms of which we possess intimate knowledge. As Nobel Prize winner Ellie Wiesel famously said, "We must take sides. Neutrality helps the oppressor, never the victim. Silence encourages the tormentor, never the tormented. Sometimes we must interfere" (The Elie Wiesel Foundation for Humanity). Our perspective is needed throughout the disciplines, and voicing critical opinions within our institutions can help us find a stronger place within academe. We need to shed our cloaks of invisibility and participate in scholarly practices ourselves for the future of librarianship to thrive.

Here is a great example for consideration from outside academic librarianship: Ten days after George Floyd's death at the hands of Minneapolis police was caught on video, G. Marcus Cole, the Joseph A. Matson Dean and Professor of Law at the University of Notre Dame, published an emotional essay. Cole shares his own heart-wrenching experience with racism as both a child and an adult. But that is only part of what makes his essay remarkable. In the end, he lays out three specific action items:

> It is urgent that we recognize that human rights are under threat all around the world, including here in the United States. This reality must be acknowledged,

and addressed. To do so, I want to restore Father Hesburgh's original vision for Notre Dame Law School by taking three steps. First, I will work with my faculty colleagues at Notre Dame to restore Father Hesburgh's vision for our Master of Laws in Human Rights. This program will continue to train lawyers from around the world, and also lawyers interested in advancing the fight for human rights here in the United States. We will fully fund students selected to train at Notre Dame Law School for a career defending civil and human rights in the United States, in the same way that we do for those training to defend human rights in other countries. Second, I will work with Notre Dame faculty, alumni, and benefactors to fully fund fellowships for, and actively recruit, exceptional applicants for our Juris Doctor program committed to the cause of civil rights. Our goal will be to provide Notre Dame lawyers for every community in this country to stand vigilant against violations of civil and human rights, wherever those threats might arise. Third, I will ask the Notre Dame Law School faculty to establish a new Exoneration Law Clinic, aimed at releasing from the criminal justice system those who are victims of prosecutorial or police misconduct. We will return fathers and mothers to their sons and daughters, particularly when their only "crime" was to be born the wrong color. (Cole 2020)

This definitive action comes less than one year into Cole's appointment as dean and is but one example of a positive step forward by an individual who has the ability to empower others and make systemic change.

Workforce

Between 2010 and 2019, the main focus of discussions on academic library employees revolved around a workforce that didn't have quite the skills needed to move into the twenty-first-century research library. Suddenly, everything we thought we needed to be prepared for the twenty-first century again came into question. For example, typically our "library as place" mentality places "maintainers" in constant conflict with "innovators." Joshua Finnell (2017) writes that

> anyone who has actually worked in a traditional library knows that, as incubators of knowledge from incunabula to e-books, libraries are just as much about maintenance as innovation. Librarians maintain "legacy systems" in all forms, from an old version of Aleph to a medieval manuscript. And herein lies the tension: the library has been and always will be a necessary balance between innovation and maintenance. ILS systems, metadata, and circulation desks all need maintenance. That really new and innovative digital curation center still needs people to maintain its staffing and infrastructure if it's going to be successful, much like innovation and business growth in the United States of America is inextricably linked to the roads and bridges supporting the transportation of goods and services.

What Finnell doesn't acknowledge is the type of maintenance required within our "library as place": shelving, preservation of print materials, digitization efforts, and the face-to-face interactions we are so famous for, as our myriad of service desks continue to require personnel on-site to complete the work. Without giving them varied skills in order to quickly move to digital or remote work, they remain at the greatest risk for economic impact and job loss.

Emotional Labor, Impostor Syndrome, and Workplace Morale

Emotional labor and impostor syndrome are new topics of research for academic librarians. Emotional labor is defined (by Google Dictionary) as the "mental activity required to manage or perform the routine tasks necessary for maintaining relationships and ensuring smooth running of a household or process, typically regarded as an unappreciated or unacknowledged burden borne disproportionately by women." Kaetrena Davis Kendrick (2017) writes that despite LIS articles focusing on workplace bullying, incivility, toxicity, and burnout, somehow we have hidden the low morale experiences that have been shared. Kendrick (2017) took a phenomenological approach in collecting and analyzing to show that

> despite the trope of academic libraries as places of quiet, comfort, and refuge, academic libraries are not immune to low morale. Academic librarians who experience low morale are often victims of long-term workplace abuse, including emotional, verbal/written abuse, system abuse, and negligence—a form of abuse that has not been widely covered in previous works on negative workplace behaviors.

As places devoted to inquiry, with people who largely focus on social justice, libraries should acknowledge the results of Kendrick's study and others and address them systematically.

Impostor syndrome, according to Merriam-Webster, is "a psychological condition characterized by a persistent doubt concerning one's abilities or accomplishments, accompanied by the fear of being exposed as a fraud despite evidence of one's ongoing success." Caitlin McClurg and Rhiannon Jones (2018) provide an "introductory exploration of how the modern Master of Library and Information Science (MLIS) may contribute to the effect of imposter phenomenon (IP) in graduate students and early career librarians and . . . offer solutions to mitigate the effect." Their results indicate that our profession is, like most others, not immune to impostor syndrome and is something that we should pay attention to, as well as conduct more research in.

Most recently, Sean P. Kennedy and Kevin R. Garewal (2020) studied workplace morale through the lens of direct leadership contact. Their findings suggest that the "workplace morale of academic librarians is predicted by several variables within a supervisor's influence including feedback, work autonomy, and supervisor qualities such as communication, transparency, and empowering subordinates" (Kennedy and Garewal 2020). Contributors to low morale included reduced staffing levels, lack of performance feedback, and lack of trust. Positive morale is possible through "recognizing exceptional work, increasing transparency, mentoring librarians, and empowering librarians" (Kennedy and Garewal 2020). The difference between this study and other similar studies is the emphasis on the relationship between "academic librarians and the academic library managers who directly supervise them," and the results are not surprising. It also serves as a great reminder of the importance of relationship building in all aspects of our roles as academic librarians.

Learning and Development

Another area that endures constant debate for definition is learning and development. Regardless of what you call it—continuing education, mentoring, networking, professional development, personal development, or professional engagement—everyone agrees it is an important component of anchoring success in academic librarianship. The debate revolves around who, when, what, and why. Some argue that professional engagement should be addressed in graduate library school programs (Rex, Whelan, and Wilson 2019); others note that it is part of contribution activities; and still others report it as personal development. This should be included in the category of topics to be clearly outlined and defined.

Recruitment and Retention of Diverse Workforce

Sojourna Cunningham, Samantha Guss, and Jennifer Stout (2019) highlight the challenges and ongoing efforts of hiring a diverse workforce. While they note some progress made in our efforts to recruit and retain a diverse workforce, their research indicates that we have some real work to do at removing obstacles at systemic levels. For example, their article cites examples in the literature of academic libraries' "institutional culture of whiteness," which can obstruct our efforts; "white centered practices"; and "racial microaggressions" (Cunningham, Guss, and Stout 2019). The authors cite feelings of isolation, experiences of racial discrimination, hostile work environments, and the isolation of a "token" minority as examples of the White institutional culture and White-centered practices. The microaggressions are found in "brief, everyday exchanges that send denigrating messages to people of color because they belong to a racial minority group" (Cunningham, Guss, and Stout 2019).

In addition, Ozlem Sensoy and Robin DiAngelo (2017) call out Whiteness "as a fundamental barrier to integration" in three ways:

> First, they tend to view diversity as a stand-alone policy that is conceptualized as the adding of students or faculty of color to the existing makeup of the institution and do not address the fundamental Whiteness of the university's policies and practices. Second, the conceptualization and implementation of diversity initiatives in this manner nearly always add workload to the most junior faculty of color and the few numbers of senior faculty of color who can mentor them. Third, diversity initiatives render their underlying logic of Whiteness invisible and thus normalize the everyday discourses that racialize only faculty of color. In these ways, the everyday "grammar of whiteness" (Bonilla-Silva, 2012) remains unaddressed.

The good news is that the authors offer constructive alternatives for consideration in the recruitment process that all of us should be incorporating into our searches. Suggestions include ensuring competitive salaries and benefits, work-life balance, professional development funds, educating employees on racial microaggressions, unconscious bias, and allyship training. We cannot continue to ignore the reality of experiences shared by our academic librarians of color.

CONCLUSION AND PROPOSALS

If there is an upside to the moment in time we find ourselves in, it is how quickly and beautifully people everywhere learned to adapt in response to uncertainty and our refusal to embrace fear. The way we identify ourselves as academic librarians now, in this moment, will determine where we go from here. Like any good research, this book started with a framework that included setting foundational definitions and a shared understanding of what we mean by words like *educational requirements*, *profession*, *professional*, *research*, *service*, and status. While there is plenty of information to be found in these definitions, it is harder to find a shared understanding. I propose the following to both continue to create that shared understanding and to keep us working toward our transformation:

1. All library school programs must include a comprehensive required course for those completing the academic library track that mirrors the notoriously more rigorous training in both research methods and the ins and outs of the academy that is built into PhD programs. Make it part of the school program accreditation process. Also include a thorough introduction to the tenure and promotion process that comes with being an academic librarian in many institutions.

2. My research found several calls for the creation of a national agenda for research libraries. Now, many of our associations have agendas (e.g., American Library Association, Association of College and Research Libraries, Association of Research Libraries, and International Federation of Library Associations and Institutions) that are for the most part siloed. We should form a task force made up of library school educators, practicing librarians, representatives from the associations that represent academic libraries, library school students, and academic library leaders to consider the future of academic librarianship. With outcomes that include the creation of standards, certification, required educational components, and agreement on how to maneuver through the paradigm shift, this is just beginning.
3. Because research is a required component for all academic librarians, how can we ensure that everyone has their own research agenda? Our library schools are making great strides by including (and in some cases requiring) research methods courses that clearly outline the research framework. What else can we do? Assign everyone a research mentor. That person's role will be to work with the new library faculty member on their contribution to scholarship, including the questions they have, what their interests are, and why; where they see needs in their field of expertise; projects; issues; broad themes; and gaps.
4. Twenty years into the current century, dealing with resistance to change doesn't seem to be resolved anytime soon. We can't lose sight of change management as a regular component of leadership competencies.
5. In our current landscape, "maintenance" and "innovation" are continually at odds with one another, competing for the same resources and prioritization. We *must* figure out how to remove the competition and embrace both as necessary anchors of our profession.
6. As long as we continue to have a variety of options for the status of academic librarians, we can commit to publishing the status of the librarians at institutions in job advertisements. Currently, that information is not always easy to find, and having that knowledge is an important decision-making factor.

Researching and reviewing nearly 150 years of information related to academic librarianship has been eye-opening to say the least. Despite where you stand on the questions proposed, researched, and responded to in this book, one thing hopefully has become crystal clear: we are on the precipice of a paradigm shift unlike anything we have ever experienced. If we care at all about the future of this profession—and the evidence shows that we do—then this is our moment in time. We face a future that is rife with both uncertainty . . . and possibility.

Bibliography

ACRL Board of Directors. 2011. "Statement on the Certification and Licensing of Academic Librarians." May 11, 2011. http://www.ala.org/acrl/standards/statementcertification.
ACRL Committee on the Status of Academic Librarians. 2007. "Guidelines for Academic Status for College and University Librarians: Approved by the ACRL Board, January 23, 2007." *College and Research Libraries News* 68, no. 6 (June): 378–79. https://crln.acrl.org/index.php/crlnews/article/view/7822/0.
ACRL Research Planning and Review Committee. 2020. "2020 Top Trends in Academic Libraries: A Review of the Trends and Issues Affecting Academic Libraries in Higher Education." *College and Research Libraries News* 81, no. 6 (June): 270. https://crln.acrl.org/index.php/crlnews/article/view/24478/32315.
ALA Forward Together. n.d.a. "SCOE Project Charge." Accessed January 23, 2021. https://forwardtogether.ala.org/index.php/about-scoe/charge/.
———. n.d.b. "Welcome." Accessed January 23, 2021. https://forwardtogether.ala.org/.
Almeida, Nora. 2018. "Interrogating the Collective: #Critlib and the Problem of Community." New York City College of Technology. https://academicworks.cuny.edu/ny_pubs/233/.
American Bar Association (ABA). n.d. "Membership FAQ." Accessed May 17, 2020. https://www.americanbar.org/membership/faq/.
American Libraries. 2018. "Are Libraries Neutral? Highlights from the Midwinter President's Program." June 1, 2018. https://americanlibrariesmagazine.org/2018/06/01/are-libraries-neutral/.
American Association of University Professors (AAUP). 2012. "Joint Statement on Faculty Status of College and University Librarians." June 2012. https://www.aaup.org/report/joint-statement-faculty-status-college-and-university-librarians.
American Library Association (ALA). n.d.a. "Education and Careers." Accessed January 19, 2021. http://www.ala.org/educationcareers/.
———. n.d.b. "Learn about Membership Types." Accessed January 23, 2021. http://www.ala.org/membership/learn-about-membership-types.
———. n.d.c. "Library Research Round Table." Accessed March 22, 2020. http://www.ala.org/rt/lrrt.
———. 2001. "Dissemination of Research in LIS." June 2001. http://www.ala.org/aboutala/offices/ors/orscommittees/dissemination/dissemination.
———. 2010. "A Guideline for the Appointment, Promotion and Tenure of Academic Librarians." June 2010. http://www.ala.org/acrl/standards/promotiontenure.
———. 2012. "Accreditation Process, Policies, and Procedures (AP3), Fourth Edition." January 31, 2012. http://www.ala.org/educationcareers/accreditedprograms/standards/AP3.

———. 2013a. "Certification and Licensure." Last modified September 2, 2013. http://www.ala.org/tools/atoz/certification-and-licensure.
———. 2013b. "Continuing Education (and Where to Find It)." Last modified September 23, 2013. http://www.ala.org/tools/atoz/continuing-education.
———. 2019a. "ALA Executive Board Releases Statement Regarding Incident at Council Forum." Press release. January 31, 2019. http://www.ala.org/news/member-news/2019/01/ala-executive-board-releases-statement-regarding-incident-council-forum.
———. 2019b. *ALA Policy Manual*. Chicago: American Library Association.
———. 2019c. "A Better ALA: A Modern Association for a Modern Profession: Preliminary Recommendations." ALA annual conference 2019. http://www.ala.org/aboutala/sites/ala.org.aboutala/files/content/governance/council/council_documents/2019_ac_docs/ALA%20CD%2045%20A%20Better%20ALA%20-%20SCOE%20Final%20-%202019.06.11%20-%20Council.pdf.
———. 2020. "ALA Appoints Tracie D. Hall as Executive Director." Press release. January 15, 2020. http://www.ala.org/news/press-releases/2020/01/ala-appoints-tracie-d-hall-executive-director.
American Library Association (ALA) Committee on Training. 1907. *Training for Librarianship*. Library Tract, no. 9. Boston: ALA Publishing Board.
American Medical Association (AMA). n.d. "AMA Membership Eligibility." Accessed May 17, 2020. https://www.ama-assn.org/member-benefits/member-eligibility-dues/ama-membership-eligibility.
Anaya, Toni, and Charlene Maxey-Harris. 2017, September. *Diversity and Inclusion: SPEC Kit 356*. Washington, DC: Association of Research Libraries. https://doi.org/10.29242/spec.356.
Anderson, Rick. 2017. "When the Wolf Finally Arrives: Big Deal Cancellations in North American Libraries." Scholarly Kitchen. May 1, 2017. https://scholarlykitchen.sspnet.org/2017/05/01/wolf-finally-arrives-big-deal-cancelations-north-american-libraries/.
Antell, Karen, and Susan E. Hahn. 2020. "Faculty Status: The Next Generation Employment Status Preferences among Millennial LIS Students and New Librarians at ARL Institutions." *Journal of Academic Librarianship* 46, no. 6 (November). https://doi.org/10.1016/j.acalib.2020.102250.
Applegate, Rachel. 1993. "Deconstructing Faculty Status: Research and Assumptions." *Journal of Academic Librarianship* 19, no. 3: 158–64.
Asheim, Lester. 1978. "Librarians as Professionals." *Library Trends* (Winter): 225–57.
Askew, Consuella A., and Eileen Theodore-Shusta. 2013. "How Do Librarians Learn Assessment?" *Library Leadership and Management* 28, no. 1 (November): 1–9.
Association of College and Research Libraries (ACRL). 1981. "Academic Status Survey." *College and Research Libraries News* 42, no. 6. https://crln.acrl.org/index.php/crlnews/article/view/19928/23762.
———. 2000. "ACRL Statement on Professional Development." *College and Research Libraries News* 61, no. 10. https://crln.acrl.org/index.php/crlnews/article/view/19978/23862.
———. 2010. "A Guideline for the Appointment, Promotion, and Tenure of Academic Librarians." June 2010. http://www.ala.org/acrl/standards/promotiontenure.
———. 2011a. "ACRL Standards for Faculty Status for Academic Librarians." October 2011. http://www.ala.org/acrl/standards/standardsfaculty.
———. 2011b. "Statement on the Terminal Professional Degree for Academic Librarians." May 11, 2011. http://www.ala.org/acrl/standards/statementterminal.
———. 2012. "ACRL Joint Statement on Faculty Status of College and University Librarians." October 2012. http://www.ala.org/acrl/standards/jointstatementfaculty.
Auld, Lawrence W. S. 1990. "Seven Imperatives for Library Education." *Library Journal* (May 1): 55–59.
Ayre, Lori Bowen. 2015. "Time to Re-Professionalize the Profession." *Collaborative Leadership* 7, no. 4: 183–85.
Ballantine, Jeanne H. 1997. *Sociology of Education: A Systematic Analysis*, 4th ed. Upper Saddle River, NJ: Prentice Hall.

Bao, Xue-Ming. 2000. "An Analysis of the Research Areas of the Articles Published in *C&RL* and *JAL* between 1990 and 1999." *College and Research Libraries* 61, no. 6 (November): 536–44.

Bell, Christina, and Marisa Mendez-Brady. 2017. "The Future of Librarianship: Challenging Professional Norms." *Journal of New Librarianship* 2: 113–16.

Bell, J. P. 2012. "Certification of Librarians: An Unproven Demand." *SLIS Student Research Journal* 2, no. 1. http://scholarworks.sjsu.edu/slissrj/vol2/iss1/3.

Berelson, Bernard, ed. 1949. *Education for Librarianship: Papers Presented at the Library Conference, University of Chicago, August 16–21, 1948.* Chicago: American Library Association.

Berry, John. 1986. "Problems of a 'Graying' Profession." *Library Journal* (November 1).

Bertot, John Carlo, Lindsay C. Sarin, and Johnna Percell. 2015. *Re-Envisioning the MLS: Findings, Issues, and Considerations.* College Park: College of Information Studies, University of Maryland. http://mls.umd.edu/wp-content/uploads/2015/08/ReEnvisioningFinalReport.pdf.

Biggs, Mary. 1981. "Sources of Tension and Conflict between Librarians and Faculty." *Journal of Higher Education* 52, no. 2 (March/April): 182–201.

Bivens-Tatum, Wayne. 2012. *Libraries and the Enlightenment.* Sacramento, CA: Library Juice Press.

Black, William K., and Joan M. Leysen. 1994. "Scholarship and the Academic Librarian." *College and Research Libraries* (May): 229–41.

Blakemore, Erin. 2018. "The Father of Modern Libraries Was a Serial Sexual Harasser." History. Last updated August 22, 2018. https://www.history.com/news/the-father-of-modern-libraries-was-a-serial-sexual-harasser.

Blecic, Deborah D., Stephen E. Wiberley Jr., Sandra L. De Groote, John Cullars, Mary Shultz, and Vivian Chan. 2017. "Publication Patterns of U.S. Academic Librarians and Libraries from 2003 to 2012." *College and Research Libraries* (May): 442–58.

Bradshaw, Agnes K. 2013. "Contrasting Professional Development and Continuing Education Opportunities for Library Professionals: Offerings Both within and outside the Profession." In *Revolutionizing the Development of Library and Information Professionals: Planning for the Future*, edited by S. S. Hines, 144–62. Hershey, PA: IGI Global

Brainard, Jeffrey. 2020. "Huge Open-Access Journal Deal Inked by University of California and Springer Nature." *Science Magazine* (June 16). https://www.sciencemag.org/news/2020/06/huge-open-access-journal-deal-inked-university-california-and-springer-nature.

Bridegam, Willis. 1978. "A Research Requirement for Librarians?" *Journal of Academic Librarianship* 4 (July): 135.

Brown, Jeanne M. 2001. "Time and the Academic Librarian." *portal: Libraries and the Academy* 1, no. 1 (January): 59–70.

Buckland, Michael K. 1998. *Library Services in Theory and Context.* 2nd ed. Oxford, UK: Pergamon Press.

———. 2003. "Five Grand Challenges for Library Research." *Library Trends* 51, no. 4 (Spring): 675–88.

Bundy, Mary L., and Paul Wasserman. 1968. "Professionalism Reconsidered." *College and Research Libraries* 29, no. 23 (January).

Butler, Pierce. 1933. *An Introduction to Library Science.* Chicago: University of Chicago Press.

———. 1951. "Librarianship as a Profession." *Library Quarterly* 21, no. 4 (October): 235–48.

Cassuto, Leonard. 2016. "University Service: The History of an Idea." MLA Profession. November 2016. https://profession.mla.org/university-service-the-history-of-an-idea/.

Chawla, Dalmeet Singh. 2020. "This Tool Is Saving Universities Millions of Dollars in Journal Subscriptions." *Science* (July 9, 2020). https://www.sciencemag.org/news/2020/07/tool-saving-universities-millions-dollars-journal-subscriptions.

Christiansen, L., M. Stombler, and L. Thaxton. 2004. "A Report on Librarian-Faculty Relations from a Sociological Perspective." *Journal of Academic Librarianship* 30: 116–21.

Coker, Catherine, Wyoma van Duinkerken, and Stephen Bales. 2010. "Seeking Full Citizenship: A Defense of Tenure Faculty Status for Librarians." *College and Research Libraries* (2010): 406–20.

Cole, G. Marcus. 2020. "I Am George Floyd. Except, I Can Breathe. And I Can Do Something." De Nicola Center for Ethics and Culture. June 5, 2020. https://ethicscenter.nd.edu/news/ndls-dean-g-marcus-cole-i-am-george-floyd-except-i-can-breathe-and-i-can-do-something/.

College Choice. n.d. Accessed January 24, 2021. https://www.collegechoice.net/.

Cosgriff, John, Donald Kenney, and Gail McMillan. 1990. "Support for Publishing at Academic Libraries: How Much Exists?" *Journal of Academic Librarianship* 16, no. 2: 94–97.

Cowley, W. H. 1928. *The Profession of Librarianship.* Washington, DC: American Council on Education.

Cox, Christopher. 2020. "Changed, Changed Utterly." Inside Higher Ed. June 5, 2020. https://www.insidehighered.com/views/2020/06/05/academic-libraries-will-change-significant-ways-result-pandemic-opinion.

Critlib. n.d. Accessed January 24, 2021. http://critlib.org/.

Cronin, Blaise. 2001. "The Mother of All Myths." *Library Journal* 15 (February): 144.

Cubberley, Carol W. 1996. *Tenure and Promotion for Academic Librarians: A Guidebook with Advice and Vignettes.* Jefferson, NC: McFarland.

Cunningham, Sojourna, Samantha Guss, and Jennifer Stout. 2019. "Challenging the 'Good Fit' Narrative: Creating Inclusive Recruitment Practices in Academic Libraries." Paper presented at the ACRL 2019 Conference, Cleveland, OH.

Damasco, Ione T., and Dracine Hodges. 2012. "Tenure and Promotion Experiences of Academic Librarians of Color." *College and Research Libraries* 73, no. 3: 279–301.

Davey, Nancy, and Theodora Andrews. 1978. "Implications of Faculty Status for University Librarians, with Special Attention to Tenure." *Journal of Academic Librarianship* 4 (May): 73–74.

DeBoer, Kee, and Wendy Culotta. 1987. "The Academic Librarian and Faculty Status in the 1980s: A Survey of the Literature." *College and Research Libraries* (May): 215–23.

Degree Query. n.d. Accessed January 24, 2021. https://www.degreequery.com/.

Deschamps, Ryan. 2010. "Ten Reasons Why 'Professional Librarian' Is an Oxymoron." *Punctuated Equilibrium: A Librarian's View of Public Policy* (blog). April 30, 2010. https://otherlibrarian.wordpress.com/2010/04/30/ten-reasons-why-professional-librarian-is-an-oxymoron/.

deSimone Watson, Paula. 1977. "Publication Activity among Academic Librarians." *College and Research Libraries* (September): 375–84.

Dewey, Barbara I. 1996. "Preparations for Librarians as Agents of Change." In *Creating the Future: Essays on Librarianship in an Age of Great Change,* edited by Sally Gardner Reed. Jefferson, NC: McFarland.

Douglass, R. R. 1957. "The Personality of the Librarian." PhD dissertation, University of Chicago.

Downs, Robert E. 1968. "Status of Academic Librarians in Retrospect." *College and Research Libraries* (July): 253–58.

Drabinski, Emily. 2016. "Valuing Professionalism: Discourse as Professional Practice." *Library Trends* 64, no. 3 (Winter): 604–14.

———. 2019. "What Is Critical about Critical Librarianship?" Special issue, *Critical Art Librarianship, Art Libraries Journal* 44, no. 2 (April): 49–57.

Dunlap, Leslie W. 1972. *Readings in Library History.* London: R. R. Bowker.

Dunn, Sydni. 2013. "As Their Roles Change, Some Librarians Lose Faculty Status." *Chronicle of Higher Education* 59, no. 28 (March 22).

England, Paula, Andrew Levine, and Emma Mishel. 2020. "Progress toward Gender Equality in the United States Has Slowed or Stalled." *Proceedings of the National Academy of Sciences of the United States of America.* March 30, 2020. https://doi.org/10.1073/pnas.1918891117.

English, Thomas G. 1983. "Librarian Status in the Eighty-Nine U.S. Academic Institutions of the Association of Research Libraries: 1982." *College and Research Libraries* 44 (May): 199–211.

Ennis, Philip H., and Howard W. Winger, eds. 1961. *Seven Questions about the Profession of Librarianship: The Twenty-Sixth Annual Conference of the Graduate Library School June 21–23, 1961.* Chicago: University of Chicago Press.

Etschmaier, Gale S., Robin N. Sinn, and Jason Priem. 2020. "Negotiating Big Deals: ACRL/SPARC Forum at the 2020 ALA Midwinter Meeting." *College and Research Libraries News* 87, no. 7: 341.

Ettarh, Fobazi. 2018. "Vocational Awe and Librarianship: The Lies We Tell Ourselves." *In the Library with the Lead Pipe* (January 10). http://www.inthelibrarywiththeleadpipe.org/2018/vocational-awe.

Fennewald, Joseph. 2008. "Research Productivity among Librarians: Factors Leading to Publications at Penn State." *College and Research Libraries* 69, no. 2: 107.

Finlay, S. Craig, Chaoqun Ni, Andrew Tsou, Cassidy R. Sugimoto. 2013. "Publish or Practice? An Examination of Librarians' Contributions to Research." *portal: Libraries and the Academy* 13, no. 4 (October): 403–21.

Finlay, S. Craig, Cassidy R. Sugimoto, Daifeng Li, and Terrell G. Russell. 2012. "LIS Dissertation Titles and Abstracts (1930–2009): Where Have All the Librar* Gone?" *Library Quarterly* 82, no. 1: 29–46.

Finnell, Joshua. 2017. "Innovators and Maintainers: Musings on Library Competencies." *Journal of New Librarianship* 1: 59–67.

Fisher, William. 1997. "The Value of Professional Associations." *Library Trends* 46, no. 2: 320–30.

Flatley, Robert K., and Michael A. Weber. 2004. "Professional Development Opportunities for New Academic Librarians." *Journal of Academic Librarianship* 30, no. 6 (November): 488–92.

Fleming-May, Rachel A., and Kimberly Douglass. 2014. "Framing Librarianship in the Academy: An Analysis Using Bolman and Deal's Model of Organizations." *College and Research Libraries* (May): 389–415.

Floyd, B. L., and J. C. Phillips. 1997. "A Question of Quality: How Authors and Editors Perceive Library Literature." *College and Research Libraries* 58: 81–93.

Floyd, Carol Everly. 1985. *Faculty Participation in Decision Making: Necessity or Luxury?* ASHE-ERIC Higher Education Reports, no. 8. Washington, DC: Association for the Study of Higher Education.

Forgotson, Jane. 1961. "A Staff Librarian Views the Problem of Status." *College and Research Libraries* 22 (July): 275–82.

Forsyth, Patrick B., and Thomas J. Danisiewicz. 1985. "Toward a Theory of Professionalization." *Work and Occupations* 12: 59–76.

Frank, Donald G. 1997. "Activity in Professional Associations: The Positive Difference in a Librarian's Career." *Library Trends* 46, no. 2 (Fall): 307–19.

Frazier, Ken. 2001. "The Librarian's Dilemma: Contemplating the Cost of the Big Deal." *D-Lib Magazine* 7, no. 3 (March). http://www.dlib.org/dlib/march01/frazier/03frazier.html.

Freedman, Shin. 2014. "Faculty Status, Tenure, and Professional Identity: A Pilot Study of Academic Librarians in New England." *portal: Libraries and the Academy* 14, no. 4 (October): 533–65.

Galbraith, Quinn, Melissa Garrison, and Whitney Hales. 2016. "Perceptions of Faculty Status among Academic Librarians." *College and Research Libraries* (September): 582–94.

Gamble, Lynne E. 1989. "University Service: New Implications for Academic Librarians." *Journal of Academic Librarianship* 14, no. 6: 344–47.

Garcia, Kenny. n.d. "Keeping Up with . . . Critical Librarianship." American Library Association. Accessed November 18, 2020. http://www.ala.org/acrl/publications/keeping_up_with/critlib.

Gillum, Shalu. 2010. "The True Benefit of Faculty Status for Academic Reference Librarians." *Reference Librarian* 51, no. 4 (October).

Gilman, Daniel Coit. 1898. "University Libraries, an Address at the Opening of the Sage Library of Cornell University, October 7, 1891." In *University Problems in the United States*, 245–55. New York: Century.

Gilman, Todd, ed. 2017. *Academic Librarianship Today.* Lanham, MD: Roman and Littlefield.

Gilman, Todd, and Thea Lindquist. 2010. "Academic/Research Librarians with Subject Doctorates: Experiences and Perceptions, 1965–2006." *portal: Libraries and the Academy* 10, no. 4 (October): 399–412.

Goode, William J. 1957. "Community within a Community: The Professions." *American Sociological Review* 22 (April): 194–200.

———. 1960. "Encroachment, Charlatanism, and the Emerging Professions: Psychology, Medicine, and Sociology." *American Sociological Review* 25: 902–14.

———. 1961. "The Librarian: From Occupation to Profession?" *Library Quarterly: Information, Community, Policy* 31, no. 4 (October): 306–20.

Grad School Hub. 2020. "Best Master's: Library Science." https://www.gradschoolhub.com/best/masters-degrees-in-library-science/.

Hathcock, April. 2015. "White Librarianship in Black Face: Diversity Initiatives in LIS. *In the Library with the Lead Pipe* (October 7). http://www.inthelibrarywiththeleadpipe.org/2015/lis-diversity.

———. 2019. "ALAMW: What Happened, and What Should Happen Next." *At the Intersection* (blog). January 30, 2019. https://aprilhathcock.wordpress.com/2019/01/30/alamw-what-happened-and-what-should-happen-next/.

Havener, W. Michael, and Wilbur A. Stolt. 1994. "The Professional Development Activities of Academic Librarians: Does Institutional Support Make a Difference?" *College and Research Libraries* (January): 25–36.

Henry, W. E. 1922. *Librarianship: A Profession*. Seattle: University of Washington Press.

Hernon, Peter. 1991. "The Elusive Nature of Research in LIS." In *Library and Information Science Research: Perspectives and Strategies for Improvement*, edited by Charles R. McClure and Peter Hernon, 3–14. Norwood, NJ: Ablex.

———. 2016. "Five Challenges Confronting Library-Related Research and Researchers." *Public Library Quarterly* 35, no. 4: 298–310. https://doi.org/10.1080/01616846.2016.1245000.

Hernon, Peter, and Candy Schwartz. 1993. "Library and Information Science: What Do We Need?" *Library and Information Science Research* (January): 115–16.

Hill, Janet Swan. 2005. "Constant Vigilance, Babelfish, and Foot Surgery: Perspectives on Faculty Status and Tenure for Academic Librarians." *portal: Libraries and the Academy* 5, no. 1 (January): 7–22.

Hinchliffe, Lisa Janicke, and Christine Wolff-Eisenberg. 2020. "Indications of the New Normal: A (Farewell) Fall 2020 Update from the Academic Library Response to COVID-19 Survey." Ithaka S+R. October 8, 2020. https://sr.ithaka.org/blog/indications-of-the-new-normal/.

Hofstadter, Richard. 1963. *Anti-Intellectualism in American Life*. New York: Knopf.

Hoggan, Danielle Bodrero. 2003. "Faculty Status for Librarians in Higher Education." *portal: Libraries and the Academy* 33, no. 3: 431–45.

Holley, Robert P. 2016. "Library Culture and the MLIS: The Bonds That Unite Librarianship." *Bottom Line* 29, no. 3: 207–17.

Hollister, Christopher V. 2016. "An Exploratory Study on Post-tenure Research Productivity among Academic Librarians." *Journal of Academic Librarianship* 42, no. 4 (July): 368–81.

Honma, Todd. 2005. "Trippin over the Color Line: The Invisibility of Race in Library and Information Studies." *InterActions: UCLA Journal of Education and Information Studies* 1, no. 2: 1–26. http://escholarship.org/ucitem/4nj0w1mp.

Horowitz, Julia. 2013. "Library Employees Protest Changed Title: New Designation for Incoming Employee Provokes Heated Debate." *Cavalier Daily*, March 7, 2013. https://www.cavalierdaily.com/article/2013/03/library-enacts-title-changes.

Hosburgh, Nathan. 2011. "Librarian Faculty Status: What Does It Mean in Academia?" *Library Philosophy and Practice* (2011): 572.

Hudson, David James. 2016. "On Critical Librarianship and Pedagogies of the Practical." Keynote presentation, Critical Librarianship and Pedagogy Symposium, Tucson, AZ, February 25–26, 2016. http://hdl.handle.net/10150/612654.

Hussey, Lisa. 2010. "The Diversity Discussion: What Are We Saying?" *Progressive Librarian* 34–35: 3–10.

Institute of Museum and Library Services (IMLS). 2013. "IMLS Library Services September 2013 Grant Announcement." http://www.imls.gov/news/2013_ols_grant_announcement.aspx.

International Federation of Library Associations (IFLA). 2019a. "About IFLA." Last updated December 10, 2019. https://www.ifla.org/about.

———. 2019b. "Advances in Artificial Intelligence." In *IFLA Trend Report*. https://trends.ifla.org/literature-review/advances-in-artificial-intelligence.

Jackson, M. G. 2000. "Image and Status: Academic Librarians and the New Professionalism." *Advances in Librarianship* 23: 93–115.

Jackson, Sidney L. 1974. *Libraries and Librarianship in the West: A Brief History*. New York: McGraw-Hill.

Joeckel, Carleton B. 1939. *Current Issues in Library Administration: Papers Presented before the Library Institute at the University of Chicago, August 1–12, 1938*. Chicago: University of Chicago Press.

Jones, Phillip J., W. Bede Mitchell, and Jean A. Major. 1998. "Academic Graduate Work in Academic Librarianship: Historicizing ACRL's Terminal Degree Statement." *Journal of Academic Librarianship* 24, no. 6 (November): 437–48.

Jones, Phillip J., and James Stivers. 2004. "Good Fences Make Bad Libraries: Rethinking Binary Constructions of Employment in Academic Libraries." *portal: Libraries in the Academy* 4, no. 1 (January): 85–104.

Joswick, Kathleen E. 1999. "Article Publication Patterns of Academic Librarians: An Illinois Case Study." *College and Research Libraries* 60, no. 4 (July): 340–49.

Kamm, Sue. 1997. "To Join or Not to Join: How Librarians Make Membership Decisions about Their Associations." *Library Trends* 46, no. 2: 295–306.

Katz, Brigit. 2019. "Melvil Dewey's Name Stripped from Top Library Award." *Smithsonian Magazine*, June 28, 2019. https://www.smithsonianmag.com/smart-news/melvil-deweys-name-stripped-top-library-award-180972514/.

Katzer, Jeffrey. 1989. "ALA and the Status of Research in Library/Information Science." *Library and Information Science Research* 11 (April–June): 83–87.

Kendrick, Kaetrena Davis. 2017. "The Low Morale Experience of Academic Librarians: A Phenomenological Study." *Journal of Library Administration* 57, no. 8: 846–78.

Kennedy, Marie R., and Kristine R. Brancolini. 2012. "Academic Librarian Research: A Survey of Attitudes, Involvement, and Perceived Capabilities." *College and Research Libraries* (September): 431–48.

Kennedy, Mary Lee. 2020, January. *Research Libraries as Catalytic Leaders in a Society in Constant Flux: A Report on the ARL-CNI Fall Forum 2019*. Washington, DC: Association of Research Libraries and Coalition for Networked Information. https://doi.org/10.29242/report.fallforum2019.

Kennedy, Sean P., and Kevin R. Garewal. 2020. "Quantitative Analysis of Workplace Morale in Academic Librarians and the Impact of Direct Supervisors on Workplace Morale." *Journal of Academic Librarianship* 46, no. 5 (September). https://doi.org/10.1016/j.acalib.2020.102191.

Kingma, Bruce R., and Gillian M. McCombs. 1995. "The Opportunity Costs of Faculty Status for Academic Librarians." *College and Research Libraries* (May): 258–64.

Kirkpatrick, Leonard H. 1947. "Another Approach to Staff Status." *College and Research Libraries* (July): 218–20.

Kortendick, James J., and Elizabeth W. Stone. 1971. *Job Dimensions and Educational Needs in Librarianship*. Chicago: American Library Association.

Krausse, Sylvia C., and Janice F. Sieburth. 1985. "Patterns of Authorship in Library Journals by Academic Librarians." *Serials Librarian* 9, no. 3: 127–38.

Kuhlman, A. F. 1938. "Librarianship as a Profession." *Peabody Journal of Education* 16, no. 2 (September): 71–80.

Lewis, Chris. 2018. *Academic Librarian Status* (blog). March 22, 2018. https://academiclibrarianstatus.wordpress.com/2018/03/22/academic-librarian-status/.

Lancour, Harold. 1957. "Preface." *Library Trends* 6, no. 2 (October): 103–4.

Leonhardt, Thomas W. 2004. "Faculty Status." *Technicalities* 24, no. 4 (July/August): 3–5.

Light, D. W., Jr., L. R. Marsden, and T. C. Corl. 1972, February. *The Impact of the Academic Revolution on Faculty Careers*. ERIC-AAHE Research Reports, no. 10. Washington, DC: American Association for Higher Education.

Lindquist, Thea, and Todd Gilman. 2008. "Academic/Research Librarians with Subject Doctorates: Data and Trends 1965–2006." *portal: Libraries and the Academy* 8, no. 1: 31–52.

Lonergan, David. 2009. "Is Librarianship a Profession?" *Community and Junior College Libraries* 15, no. 2: 119–22.

Long, Chris Evin, and Rachel Applegate. 2008. "Bridging the Gap in Digital Library Continuing Education: How Librarians Who Were Not 'Born Digital' Are Keeping Up." *Library Administration and Management* 22, no. 4: 172–82. https://journals.tdl.org/llm/index.php/llm/issue/view/112.

Lowry, Charles B. 1993. "The Status of Faculty Status for Academic Libraries: A Twenty-Year Perspective." *College and Research Libraries* 54 (March): 163–72.

Lundy, Frank A. 1951. "Faculty Rank for Professional Librarians," *College and Research Libraries* (January): 11–19.

Luo, Lili, and Margaret McKinney. 2015. "JAL in the Past Decade: A Comprehensive Analysis of Academic Library Research." *Journal of Academic Librarianship* 41: 123–29.

Lynch, Beverly P. 2008. "Library Education: Its Past, Its Present, Its Future." *Library Trends* 56, no. 4 (Spring): 931–53.

Maloy, Miriam C. 1939. "Faculty Status of College Librarians." *ALA Bulletin* 33 (April): 232–33, 302.

Marcum, Deanna B. 1997. "Transforming the Curriculum; Transforming the Profession." *American Libraries* 28, no. 1 (January): 35–38.

Massman, Virgil F. 1972. *Faculty Status for Librarians*. Metuchen, NJ: Scarecrow Press.

McAnally, Arthur M. 1957. "The Dynamics of Securing Academic Status." *College and Research Libraries* 18 (September): 386–95.

McClure, Charles R., and Peter Hernon. 1991. *Library and Information Science Research: Perspectives and Strategies for Improvement*. Norwood, NJ: Ablex.

McClurg, Caitlin, and Rhiannon Jones. 2018. "Imposter Phenomenon and the MLIS." In *Re-envisioning the MLS: Perspectives on the Future of Library and Information Science Education*, edited by Johnna Percell, Lindsay C. Sarin, Paul T. Jaeger, and John Carlo Bertot, 7–24. Advances in Librarianship, vol. 44A. Bingley, UK: Emerald.

McMillen, James A. 1924. "College and Reference Section." *Bulletin of the American Library Association* 18 (August): 305–8. https://www.jstor.org/stable/25686311?seq=2#metadata_info_tab_contents.

———. 1940. "Academic Status of Library Staff Members of Large Universities." *College and Research Libraries* 1 (March): 138–40.

Mitchell, Robert. 2018. "Andrew Carnegie Built 1,700 Public Libraries. But Some Towns Refused the Steel Baron's Money." *Washington Post*, April 9, 2018. https://www.washingtonpost.com/news/retropolis/wp/2018/04/09/andrew-carnegie-built-1700-public-libraries-but-some-towns-refused-the-steel-barons-money/.

Mitchell, W. Bede, and Mary Reichel. 1999. "Publish or Perish: A Dilemma for Academic Librarians?" *College and Research Libraries* 60, no. 3 (May 1): 232–43.

Montanelli, Dale S., and Patricia F. Stenstrom. 1986. "The Benefits of Research for Academic Librarians and the Institutions They Serve." *College and Research Libraries* (September): 482–85.

Montelongo, José A., Lynne Gamble, Navjit Brar, and Anita C. Hernandez. 2010. "Being a Librarian Isn't Enough: The Importance of a Nonlibrary Research Agenda for the Academic Librarian: A Case Study." *College and Undergraduate Libraries* 17, no. 1: 2–19.

Moriarty, John H. 1970. "Academic in Deed." *College and Research Libraries* 31, no. 1: 14–17.

Morrison, Perry D. 1969. *The Career of the Academic Librarian*. Chicago: American Library Association.

Mortimer, Roger, and Nelson Beck. 1979. "The Librarian's Role—Two Views." *Journal of Academic Librarianship* (January): 448–50.

Mukherjee, A. K. 1966. *Librarianship, Its Philosophy and History.* Bombay: Asia Publishing House.
Mullins, James L. 2012. "Are MLS Graduates Being Prepared for the Changing and Emerging Roles That Librarians Must Now Assume within Research Libraries?" *Journal of Library Administration* 52, no. 1: 124–32.
Neal, James G. 2006a. "Raised by Wolves: Integrating the New Generation of Feral Professionals into the Academic Library." *Library Journal* (February 15): 42–44.
———. 2006b. "The Research and Development Imperative in the Academic Library: Path to the Future." *portal: Libraries and the Academy* 6, no. 1: 1–3.
Newhouse, Rita, and April Spisak. 2004. "Fixing the First Job: New Librarians Speak Out on Problems in the Profession." *Library Journal* 129, no. 13 (August): 44–46.
Nicholson, Karen P., and Maura Seale, eds. 2018. *The Politics of Theory and the Practice of Critical Librarianship.* Sacramento, CA: Library Juice Press.
Nussbaumer, A. 2005. "Door #1: Certification. Door #2: Not! Door #3: Real Solutions." In *Last One Out Turn off the Lights: Is This the Future of American and Canadian Libraries?* edited by S. E. Cleyle and L. M. McGillis, 138–50. Lanham, MD: Scarecrow Press.
Osterman, Anne C., Sophie Rondeau, Jessica Bowdoin, Genya M. O'Gara, and James Pape. 2020. "The Impact of Big Deal Breaks on Library Consortia: An Exploratory Case Study." *Serials Librarian* 79, nos. 1–2: 153–62.
Oud, Joanne. 2008. "Adjusting to the Workplace: Transitions Faced by New Academic Librarians." *College and Research Libraries* 69, no. 3 (May): 252–66.
Pagowsky, Nicole, and Miriam Rigby, eds. 2014. *The Librarian Stereotype: Deconstructing Perceptions and Presentations of Information Work.* Chicago: American Library Association.
Parker, Ralph H., and Agnes I. Reagan. 1961. "Ports of Entry to Librarianship." *Library Quarterly: Information, Community, Policy* 31, no. 4 (October): 344–55.
Pavalko, Ronald M. 1988. *Sociology of Occupations and Professions*, 2nd ed. Itasca, IL: F. E. Peacock.
Paylore, Patricia. 1957. "Heart of the Matter." *Wilson Library Bulletin* 31 (February): 455–58.
Peet, Lisa. 2020. "Lisa Janicke Hinchliffe and Christine Wolff-Eisenberg on the Final Ithaka Academic Library COVID-19 Response Survey Results." *Library Journal* (October 22).
Percell, Johnna, Lindsay C. Sarin, Paul T. Jaeger, and John Carlo Bertot. 2018. Introduction to *Re-envisioning the MLS: Perspectives on the Future of Library and Information Science Education*, edited by Johnna Percell, Lindsay C. Sarin, Paul T. Jaeger, and John Carlo Bertot, 1–5. Advances in Librarianship, vol. 44A, 1–5. Bingley, UK: Emerald.
Perkins, Gay Helen, and Amy J. W. Slowik. 2013. "The Value of Research in Academic Libraries." *College and Research Libraries* (March): 143–57.
Peters, Alison. 2016. "On the MLIS: Why I'm Getting the Library Degree." Book Riot. April 6, 2016. https://bookriot.com/mlis-rules-why-im-getting-the-library-degree/.
Pfeifer, Heather L. 2016. "How to Be a Good Academic Citizen: The Role and Importance of Service in Academia." *Journal of Criminal Justice Education* 27, no. 2: 238–54.
Powell, Ronald R., Lynda M. Baker, and Joseph J. Mika. 2002. "Library and Information Science Practitioners and Research." *Library and Information Science Research* 24: 49–72.
Prentice, Ann E. 1992. "Professional Programs in the University: A View from Not Quite the Top." *Journal of Education for Library and Information Science* 33, no. 4 (Fall): 284–86.
Rayman, Ronald, and Frank William Goudy. 1980. "Research and Publication Requirements in University Libraries." *College and Research Libraries* 41 (January): 43–48.
Rex, Jared Andrew, Jennifer L. A. Whelan, and Laura L. Wilson. 2019. "Tenure Not Required: Recasting Non-Tenured Academic Librarianship to Center Stage." In *Recasting the Narrative: The Proceedings of the ACRL 2019 Conference*, edited by Dawn M. Mueller, 439–58. Chicago: Association of College and Research Libraries.
Ridley, Michael. 2018. "Academic Librarians and the PhD." *Partnership: The Canadian Journal of Library and Information Practice and Research* 13, no. 1.
Roberts, Keith A., and Karen A. Donahue. 2012. "Professing Professionalism: Bureaucratization and Deprofessionalization in the Academy." *Sociological Focus* 33, no. 4: 365–83.

Rothstein, Samuel. 1985. "The 97-Year-Old Mystery Solved at Last: Why People Really Hate Library Schools." *Library Journal* 110, no. 6 (April 1): 41–48.

Rubin, Richard E. 2016. *Foundations of Library and Information Science*. 4th ed. Chicago: ALA Neal-Schuman.

Rudolph, Frederick. 1962. *The American College and University: A History*. New York: Knopf.

Sapon-White, Richard, Valery King, and Anne Christie. 2004. "Supporting a Culture of Scholarship for Academic Librarians." *portal: Libraries and the Academy* 4, no. 3 (July): 407–21.

Sare, Laura, Stephen Bales, and Bruce Neville. 2020. "New Academic Librarians and Their Perceptions of the Profession." *portal: Libraries and the Academy* 12, no. 2 (April): 179–203.

Sawtelle, H. A. 1878. "The College Librarianship." *Library Journal* 3 (June): 162.

Schlesselman-Tarango, Gina. 2016. "The Legacy of Lady Bountiful: White Women in the Library." *Library Trends* 64, no. 4 (Spring): 667–86.

Schmidt, Jane. 2018. "Innovate This! Bullshit in Academic Libraries and What We Can Do about It." Keynote address at CAPAL18, May 29, 2018.

Scholarly Publishing and Academic Resources Coalition (SPARC). n.d. Accessed January 20, 2021. https://sparcopen.org/.

Seale, Maura. 2016. "Institutionalizing Critical Librarianship." Presentation at the Critical Librarianship and Pedagogy Symposium, Tucson, AZ, February 25–26, 2016. http://arizona.openrepository.com/arizona/handle/10150/609829.

Sensoy, Ozlem, and Robin DiAngelo. 2017. "We Are All for Diversity, but . . . : How Faculty Hiring Committees Reproduce Whiteness and Practical Suggestions for How They Can Change." *Harvard Educational Review* 87, no. 4: 557–80.

Shaffer, Christopher. 2011. "Best Practices for Hiring Academic Librarians with Faculty Status and Rank." *Southeastern Librarian* 59, no. 3: 3–9.

Shaffer, Dale E. 1968. *The Maturity of Librarianship as a Profession*. Metuchen, NJ: Scarecrow Press.

Shiflett, Orvin Lee. 1981. *Origins of American Academic Librarianship*. Norwood, NJ: Ablex.

Silva, Elise, Quinn Galbraith, and Michael Groesbeck. 2017. "Academic Librarians' Changing Perceptions of Faculty Status and Tenure." *College and Research Libraries* 78, no. 4 (May): 428–41.

Sloniowski, Lisa. 2016. "Affective Labor, Resistance, and the Academic Librarian." *Library Trends* 64, no. 4 (Spring): 645–66.

Stone, Elizabeth W. 1969. *Factors Related to the Professional Development of Librarians*. Metuchen, NJ: Scarecrow Press.

Sugimoto, Cassidy R., Andrew Tsou, Sara Naslund, Alexandra Hauser, Melissa Brandon, Danielle Winter, Cody Behles, and S. Craig Finlay. 2014. "Beyond Gatekeepers of Knowledge: Scholarly Communication Practices of Academic Librarians and Archivists at ARL Institutions." *College and Research Libraries* (March): 145–61.

Swigger, Boyd Keith. 2010. *The MLS Project: An Assessment after 60 Years*. Lanham, MD: Scarecrow Press.

Tauber, Maurice F. 1957. "Introduction." *Library Trends* 6, no. 2 (October): 105–9.

Tewksbury, Donald George. (1932) 1965. *The Founding of American Colleges and Universities before the Civil War, with Particular Reference to the Religious Influences Bearing upon the College Movement*. Hamden, CT: Archon Books.

Thomas, Susan E., and Anne E. Leonard. 2014. "Interdisciplinary Librarians: Self-Reported Non-LIS Scholarship and Creative Work." *Library Management* 35, nos. 8–9: 547–57.

University of California, Los Angeles (UCLA). 2019. "UC Terminates Subscriptions with Elsevier in Push for Open Access." Press release. February 28, 2019. https://newsroom.ucla.edu/releases/uc-terminates-subscriptions-with-elsevier.

US Department of Education. 1988. *Rethinking the Library in the Information Age*. Vol. 3: *Building an Infrastructure for Library Research*. Washington, DC: US Department of Education, Office of Library Programs.

Veaner, Allen B. 1994. "Paradigm Lost, Paradigm Regained? A Persistent Personnel Issue in Academic Librarianship, II." *College and Research Libraries* (September): 389–402.

Vilz, Amy J., and Molly Dahl Poremski. 2015. "Perceptions of Support Systems for Tenure-Track Librarians." *College and Undergraduate Libraries* 22, no. 2: 149–66.
Wallace, Danny P. 2007. "Academic Library and Research in the Twenty-First Century: Linking Practice and Research." *Journal of Academic Librarianship* 33, no. 5: 529–31.
Walters, William H. 2016. "Faculty Status of Librarians at U.S. Research Universities." *Journal of Academic Librarianship* 42, no. 2 (March): 161–71. http://dx.doi.org/10.1016/j.acalib.2015.11.002.
Watkins, C. 1998. "Chapter Report: The Many Faces of Certification." *American Libraries* 29, no. 9: 11.
Weng, Cathy, and David Murray. 2019. "Faculty Perceptions of Librarians and Library Services: Exploring the Impact of Librarian Faculty Status and Beyond." In *Recasting the Narrative: The Proceedings of the ACRL 2019 Conference*, edited by Dawn M. Mueller, 200–210. Chicago: Association of College and Research Libraries.
Wheatley, Amanda, and Sandy Hervieux. 2019. "Artificial Intelligence in Academic Libraries: An Environmental Scan." *Information Services and Use* 39: 347–56.
White, Carl M. 1976. *A Historical Introduction to Library Education: Problems and Progress to 1951*. Metuchen, NJ: Scarecrow Press.
Wiberley, Stephen E., Jr., Julie M. Hurd, and Ann C. Weller. 2006. "Publication Patterns of U.S. Academic Librarians from 1998 to 2002." *College and Research Libraries* 67, no. 3 (May): 205–16.
Williamson, Charles C. 1923. *Training for Library Service: A Report Prepared for the Carnegie Corporation of New York*. New York: Carnegie.
Wilson, Anthony M., and Robert Hermanson. 1998. "Educating and Training Library Practitioners: A Comparative History with Trends and Recommendations." *Library Trends* 46, no. 3 (Winter): 467–504.
Winter, Michael F. 1983. *The Professionalization of Librarianship*. Occasional Papers, no. 160. Urbana: University of Illinois.
Wise, Mary. 2012. "Participation in Local Library Associations: The Benefits to Participants." Faculty Scholarship from the Library. Paper 12. http://digitalcommons.cwu.edu/libraryfac/12.
Works, George Alan. 1927. *College and University Library Problems: A Study of Selected Group of Institutions Prepared for the Association of American Universities*. Chicago: American Library Association.
Wyatt, James F. 1978. "Defining 'Academic' Librarianship." *Journal of Academic Librarianship* 4, no. 3 (July): 132–34.
Wyss, Paul Alan. 2010. "Library School Faculty Member Perceptions Regarding Faculty Status for Academic Librarians." *College and Research Libraries* (July): 375–88.

Index

American Association of University Professors, 17
American Library Association (ALA), 47–50, 53–54; and certification, 66–67; transformation of, 49, 53–54
American Library Association's Committee on Training, 60–61
American Medical Association, 7–8, 48
artificial intelligence (AI), 76–78
Association of College and Research Libraries, 17–23, 29

big deals and open access, 78–81

Canadian Association of Professional Academic Librarians, 11
Carnegie, Andrew, 2
Congress on Professional Education (CoPE), 32
COVID-19, 82–83
critical librarianship, 81–82

Derrida, Jacques, 12
Dewey, Melville, 2, 14

education for academic librarians, 60; accreditation, 65–66; certification, 67–68; professional expectations and academic expectations, 64–65; review of current MLS programs, 68–73; struggles with beginning, 61–65

educational qualifications and status of the professional librarian in colleges and universities, 20
emotional labor, 86

Foucault, Michel, 12
framework, 1–2

higher education in America and librarianship, 57–58
history of libraries, 3

imposter syndrome, 86

labor theory, 11–2
learning and development, 87
librarianship, profession, 3–10

Master of Library Science as terminal degree, 23–24
morale, 86

National Center for Education Statistics, 38
National Education Association, 17

perceptions and stereotypes of librarians, 19–20
professionalization, 10–11, 58–60
promotion and tenure, 29, 46–47

race and power systems, 14, 83–85
recruitment and retention of diverse workforce, 87–88
research in library and information science, 30; decline in publication, 37–39; identifying a research agenda, 40–41; impact of the non library research agenda, 39–40; influence of ALA, 31–33; increasing research strategies, 33–35; issues related to scarcity of, 30; limited value of, 29; research motivations, 35–37

service to the profession, 43–47; choosing not to join, 48–49; international, regional, and state organizations, 50–51; nonlibrary professional associations, 52–53; service in professional associations, 51–52

social justice, 2
standards for faculty status for college and university librarians, 22
status of academic librarians, 18–27; elements in definition of, 20–22; retrospective of, 24–27

titles, academic librarians, 18

US Bureau of Education Special Report, 18
University of Maryland's i-School Review, 72–73

vocational awe, 13

workforce, 85–86

About the Author

Marcy Simons is the organizational development librarian at the University of Notre Dame. Her path in the profession has allowed her to learn staff roles from the ground up—a leadership role as head of access services and now a faculty role, where she has the privilege of working with the senior leadership team to build leaders, create learning opportunities for faculty and staff, ensure organizational effectiveness through continuous improvement efforts, and steward organizational design. A change champion, player's coach, and certified Six Sigma Green Belt, Marcy is passionate about living her mantra of "being the change."

www.ingramcontent.com/pod-product-compliance
Lightning Source LLC
Chambersburg PA
CBHW021853300426
44115CB00005B/138